Learn to Sew

25 QUICK AND EASY SEWING PROJECTS TO GET YOU STARTED

Emma Hardy

CICO BOOKS
LONDON NEW YORK

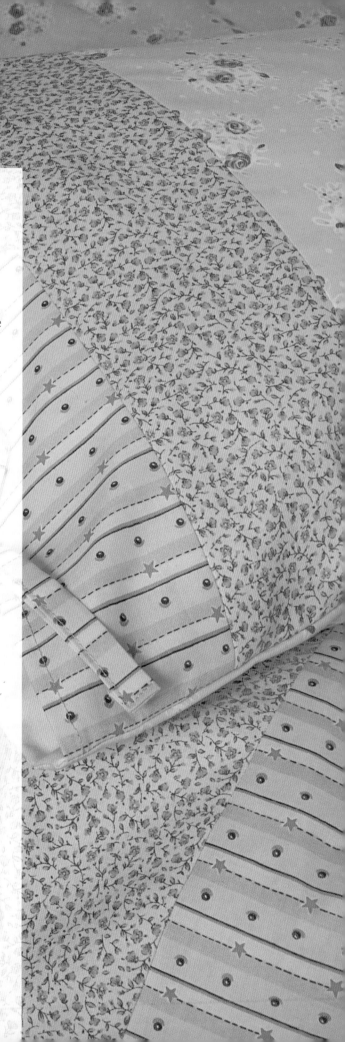

Published in 2016 by CICO Books
An imprint of Ryland Peters & Small Ltd
20–21 Jockey's Fields, London WC1R 4BW
341 E 116th St, New York, NY 10029

www.rylandpeters.com

Projects in this book have previously been published in the
titles *Sewing in No Time* and *Quilting in No Time*.

10 9 8 7 6 5 4 3 2 1

A CIP catalog record for this book is available from the
Library of Congress and the British Library.

ISBN: 978 1 78249 397 6

Printed in China

Designer: Alison Fenton
Photographer: Debbie Patterson
Stylist: Emma Hardy
Illustrator: Michael Hill

Art director: Sally Powell
Production controller: David Hearn
Publishing manager: Penny Craig
Publisher: Cindy Richards

Contents

Introduction

I have always loved sewing and have been making things for as long as I can remember. I enjoy being able to stitch projects for my home and for friends and family that I know are unique and personal to me. With the huge range of fabrics, ribbons, buttons, and braids now available to us from sewing stores and the many online companies, there has never been a better or more exciting time to learn to sew.

If you are just starting out, learning to sew can feel a little daunting but you can easily pick up the basics, enabling you to make all sorts of beautiful things. I am sure that you will discover how much more satisfying it is to furnish your home with hand-made items rather than shop-bought.

In this book, you will find 25 easy-to-make projects, all suitable for beginners. There is a handy techniques section at the start, to guide you through and help you master the basics, with ideas for putting together your own sewing kit. Each project has a materials list and is beautifully illustrated with step-by-step instructions that are easy to follow.

I hope that you will enjoy learning to sew and that you will feel inspired to design and create your own projects using the skills that you have learnt. There really will be no stopping you!

A note on measurements: all instructions in this book contain both standard (imperial) and metric measurements. Please use only one set of measurements when cutting out and sewing, as they are not interchangeable.

Techniques

The sewing techniques used in this book are all very simple, allowing you to create stylish soft furnishings and accessories for your home quickly and easily. You will need only minimal equipment for the projects in this book. It is a good idea to put together a basic sewing kit (see box, right) before you start, so that you have everything you will need close to hand.

Using templates and patterns

Several of the projects in this book require you to make a template or pattern that you can draw around to cut out a corresponding fabric shape.

Making a template

To make a template for a fabric shape, first enlarge (or reduce) your chosen motif to the size you want, or as specified on the template artwork.

1 Using a thick black pencil, trace the motif onto tracing paper.

2 Turn the tracing paper over, place it on card, and scribble over your drawn lines to transfer them to the card.

3 Finally, cut out the card shape using scissors or a craft knife on a cutting mat. You can now place the card template on your chosen fabric and draw around it with tailor's chalk or a fabric marker pencil to transfer the shape to the fabric.

Choosing fabrics

Visiting a fabric shop or browsing online for fabrics is one of the most enjoyable parts of any sewing project. For beginners, cotton and linen fabrics are simplest to use, and cotton in particular is relatively inexpensive. In projects where more than one design or color is used, it is best to buy different designs in the same kind of fabric, rather than mixing a cotton with a wool or synthetic fabric. Avoid stretch and woven fabrics for your first projects, as these are harder to handle. Finally, bear the pattern in mind—smaller patterns or plain fabric will not show the joins as much as large checks and prints.

Hand sewing

Hand sewing can be either temporary—when it is known as basting (or tacking) and is used to hold sections together while you are constructing seams—or permanent, used when the garment pieces need to be sewn together invisibly. If you are left-handed, reverse the direction of stitching given in these instructions, and work from left to right.

Securing your thread

Whether your hand sewing is temporary or permanent, you will need to secure the end of the thread when you start stitching. This can be done with a knot tied in the end of the thread or by making a couple of backstitches.

SECURING WITH BACKSTITCH

Bring the needle and thread to the upper side of the fabric at A. Insert the needle through all the fabric layers at B, one stitch length behind A, and bring it back up again at A. Repeat to form another backstitch in the same place. Trim the thread end.

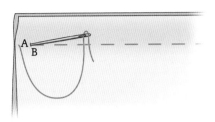

Basting

Working from right to left, take evenly spaced stitches about ¼ in (6mm) long through the fabric layers, sewing close to the seamline but within the seam allowance. Take several stitches onto your needle at one time, before drawing the thread through the fabric.

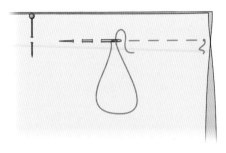

Running stitch

This is worked just like even basting stitch (see above right), except that the stitches are smaller. Running stitch is mainly used for hand gathering, though it can also be used as a decorative stitch.

Thread your needle and secure the thread. Working from right to left, weave the needle in and out of the fabric, taking several stitches onto the needle before drawing the thread through.

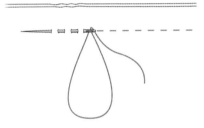

Backstitch

Thread your needle and secure the thread. Working from right to left, bring the needle and thread through to the front of the fabric. Insert the needle at A, ¹⁄₁₆–⅛in. (2–3mm) to the right of the point where it emerged, and bring it up at B, the same distance to the left of the point where it originally emerged. Draw the thread through and repeat, inserting the needle again the same distance to the right of where it has just emerged, and continue in this way along the line.

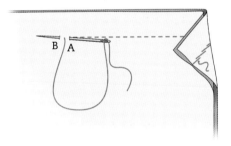

Slipstitch

Thread the needle and secure the thread. Working from right to left, bring the needle through one folded edge, slip the needle through the fold of the opposite edge for about ¼in. (6mm), and draw the needle and thread through. Continue in this way to join both edges.

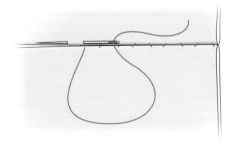

Machine sewing

Stitching plain seams

Most seams are sewn with a straight stitch on your machine. The most popular is the plain seam, in which the seam allowances are pressed open. To stop a seam from splitting open, you will need to secure the ends of the stitching at the start and finish of each seam, either by reverse stitching, which is the stronger method, or by tying the thread ends together, which gives a neater, flatter finish. Here is how to stitch a simple seam using each of these methods.

SIMPLE SEAM SECURED WITH REVERSE STITCHING

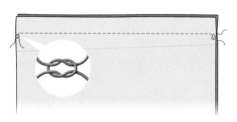

Pin and then baste the fabric pieces, then place them under the machine foot, lining up the raw edges with the correct seam guideline. Position the needle on the seamline about ½in. (1.2cm) from the top edge, and lower the presser foot. Set your machine to reverse, and then stitch backward, almost to the top edge. Change the setting to stitch forward, and stitch along the seamline to the lower edge, keeping the raw edges on the guideline. Set the machine to reverse once again and stitch backward for ½in. (1.2cm) up the seamline. Cut the threads close to the stitching.

Note: In this diagram we show the reverse stitching alongside the forward stitching, but this is only to make it visible in the diagram. Reverse stitching is actually done in line with the forward stitching.

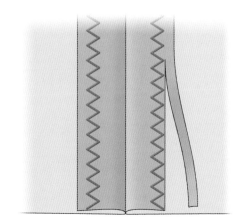

SIMPLE SEAM SECURED WITH TIED ENDS

Pin and baste the fabric pieces together, then place them under the machine foot, lining up the raw edges with the correct seam guideline. Leaving long thread ends at the top edge, stitch along the seamline from top to bottom. Cut the threads, leaving long ends. At one end, pull on the upper thread to bring a loop of the lower thread to the top of the fabric; use a pin to pull the lower thread through completely, and then tie the ends together in a square (reef) knot. Repeat at the other end of the seamline and cut off the excess thread.

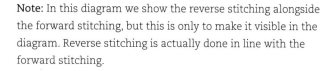

Zigzag stitch

This machine stitch can be used on most woven fabrics. It is the fastest way to finish a raw edge, leaving it neat and flat. As well as seam allowances, it is suitable for other raw edges, such as hems or the edges of any facing.

Using the normal zigzag foot, stitch on a scrap of your fabric before you begin, to double-check the stitch tension and make sure that it doesn't roll up the fabric edges.

Set your stitch for a medium-width and short-length zigzag, then stitch ⅛in. (3mm) from the edge of the seam allowance. Trim away the outer edge of the fabric, close to the zigzag stitching.

Machine gathering

Machine gathering is done by stitching two rows of long machine stitches along the edge to be gathered, within the seam allowances. The fabric is then gathered up by pulling on the bobbin threads.

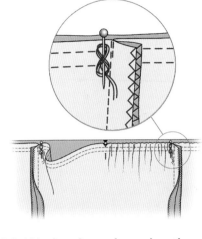

1 Leaving long thread ends, work two parallel rows of gathering stitches ¼in. (6mm) apart within the seam allowance along your fabric edge, with the outer row of stitching a thread's width from the seamline. Do not stitch over seams—stitch between any seams where necessary.

2 At one end, secure the bobbin threads by twisting them around a pin in a figure eight.

At the other end, pull both bobbin threads together and gently ease the gathers along the threads. When the gathered edge fits the piece of fabric it is to be attached to, secure the thread ends around another pin, as before. On long edges, gather the fabric from each end toward the center, rather than trying to gather across the entire piece all at once.

Machine-stitching buttonholes

Most modern machines have built-in mechanisms that stitch buttonholes either semi-automatically or fully automatically, so there is no need for you to change the needle position or to pivot your fabric manually. However, older sewing machines may ask you to hand-guide the buttonhole, so please check your manual.

WORKING A SEMI-AUTOMATIC BUTTONHOLE

A semi-automatic or sliding buttonhole foot has a gauge down the left-hand side to measure the buttonhole length. The length of the buttonhole for either a sew-through button or a shank button is determined by the diameter and height of the button. Add them together, then add an extra ⅛in. (3mm), which allows for the bar tacks at each end. Before stitching you will need to mark your buttonhole position and move the slide so that the lower mark on the slider is even with the start of the buttonhole marking on your garment. Draw both threads to the left under the foot.

1 Set your machine to the first stage of the buttonhole; you may have to turn your stitch selector or press a memory button on your machine to stitch each part of the buttonhole, so check your manual. Start the stitching—the machine will make the first bar tack (the end stitching across the whole width of the buttonhole). Stitch backward up the left-hand side of the buttonhole, stopping at the top mark.

2 Press the memory button or move your dial to stitch the next bar tack.

3 Finally, stitch down the remaining side of the buttonhole.

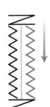

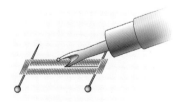

4 Place a pin at each end of the buttonhole just before the bar tacks, to protect them. Using a seam ripper, carefully slit down the center of the buttonhole between the pins.

Topstitching

Topstitching consists of rows of machine stitching done from the right side of the fabric, after the seam has been sewn. It can be functional as well as decorative—for example, to hold seam allowances flat, or to attach a pocket.

TOPSTITCHING A SEAM

Single topstitching consists of one row of stitching, usually worked parallel to a seam or an edge. Double topstitching consists of two rows of stitching, one on each side of a seamline, placed at equal distances from it.

For single topstitching, finish the seam allowances on a plain seam, and press them both to the side you are going to topstitch. Working from the right side, stitch down the side of the seamline, using the presser foot or an alternative method to keep the stitching the same distance from the seamline, and sewing through both seam allowances at the same time.

For double topstitching, press the seam allowances open, then topstitch down both sides of the seam, always stitching in the same direction and stitching through the seam allowances at the same time.

TOPSTITCHING AROUND A FINISHED EDGE

Topstitching is often done around a finished edge—as well as being decorative, it prevents the underside of the edge from rolling to the outside.

Working from the right side, line up your finished seam edge on the chosen guideline and begin stitching at a raw edge, turning any corners by lifting the presser foot and pivoting your fabric around the needle. Trim your threads ends even with the raw edges.

Box stitching

Box stitching is stitching in a square shape, with a diagonal cross in the center, to reinforce a join. It is done in one operation without removing the work to change direction.

Starting at one edge, machine stitch across the width of your elastic or strap, then continue stitching around to form a square, finishing at the starting point with the needle down. Pivot the work around the needle and stitch diagonally across the square to the opposite corner, then along the side of the square following the first line of stitching, and finally diagonally across the square to the opposite corner. To really reinforce the stitching, stitch around the square one more time. Remove the work from the machine and cut the threads.

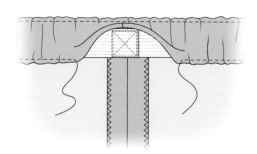

Trimming seams and corners

When several layers of fabric have been stitched, you can end up with as many as four layers of fabric, making the seam very thick and bulky. Trimming the seam allowances and corners as shown below reduces this thickness.

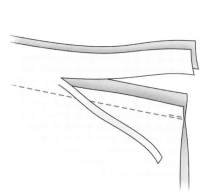

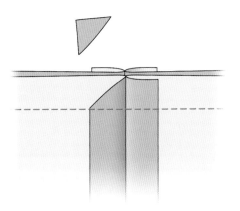

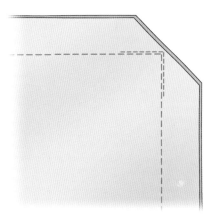

Grading seams

Also known as layering seams, grading involves trimming the seam allowances to graduated widths so that the narrowest seam allowance is ³⁄₁₆in. (5mm) wide and the widest lies next to the most visible seam edge, such as the top collar. If you are using a fabric that frays, don't trim too closely.

Trimming matched seams

Trim away the fabric corners within the seam allowance after you have stitched the seam, as shown.

Trimming a right-angled outward corner

To create a sharp, neat angle, cut across the corner of the seam allowances, as shown, close to the stitching, but making sure that you do not cut through the actual stitching. When turning your seam to the right side, use a pair of small, pointed scissors or a knitting needle to carefully push out the point, making sure you do not push too hard and form a hole.

Trimming an acute corner

This type of corner needs a little more fabric trimmed away. Cut across the corner of the seam allowances close to the stitching, as for the right-angled outward corner, then trim away another sliver of fabric from each side, as shown.

Notching or clipping curved seams

Notches are small wedges of fabric cut from the seam allowances of outward curves, as shown here, to allow them to lie smooth and flat. On inward curves you only need to clip (make snips) into the seam allowances to permit the edges to spread out and lie flat. Use a sharp pair of small, pointed scissors to notch or clip the curve at regular intervals, taking care to cut close to, but not through, the stitches.

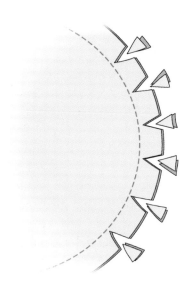

Making a hem

The hem is a sewing basic that gives a neat finish to a raw fabric edge. A hem can either be machine-stitched or hand-stitched.

Machine-stitched hems

Fold the raw hem edge over to the wrong side by ⅜in. (1cm) and pin it in place. Press along the folded edge, taking care not to press on the pins, and removing them as you go. Fold again along the hemline. Pin and baste the pressed edge in place. Press the hemline fold, then machine stitch the hem in place close to the first pressed edge. Unpick the basting stitches and give the hem a final press.

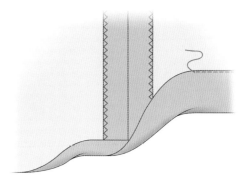

Hand-stitched hems

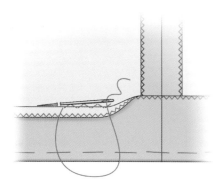

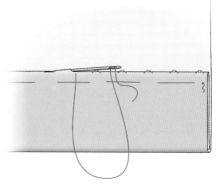

BLIND HEMMING

These hand stitches are taken inside the hem so that no stitches are visible on the right side. Also known as blindstitch, this is a quick and easy stitch that can be used on any flat hem with a finished edge.

Finish the edge to be hemmed with zigzag stitch. Pin and baste the hem in place close to the folded hem edge. With the hem allowance on top, work from right to left with the needle pointing to the left (reverse this if you are left-handed). Fold back the top edge of the hem allowance and fasten the thread just inside it. About ¼in. (6mm) to the left take a very small stitch in the garment (no more than two or three threads), then take the next stitch ¼in. (6mm) to the left in the hem allowance. Continue in this manner, keeping the stitches even and alternating them between the garment and the hem, until your hem is secured in place. Remove the basting stitches.

SLIP HEMMING

Slip hemming by hand is used to secure a folded hem edge in place, and is most commonly used for hemming curtains. This small, neat stitch is also known as uneven slipstitch and is almost invisible on the right side of your work.

Press the hem allowances to the wrong side, then pin and baste them in place. Working from the right to the left (reverse this if you are left-handed), secure the thread on the inside of the hem fabric, then bring the needle out through the hem fold. Opposite, in the garment or curtain, take a very small stitch (no more than two or three threads). Take the needle back into the folded edge and run the needle inside the fold for approximately ⅜in. (1cm). Bring the needle out and draw the thread through. Continue in this way alternating the stitches between the fabric and the fold. Make sure the stitches are not pulled too tightly or the fabric will pucker on the right side.

Fastenings

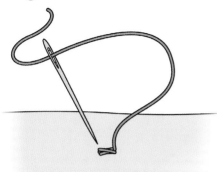

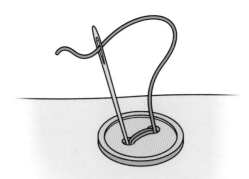

Sewing on buttons

1 Mark the place where you want the button to go. Push the needle up from the back of the fabric and sew a few stitches over and over in this place.

2 Now bring the needle up through one of the holes in the button. Push the needle back down through the second hole and through the fabric. Bring it back up through the first hole. Repeat this five or six times. If there are four holes in the button, use all four of them to make a cross pattern. Make sure that you keep the stitches close together under the middle of the button.

3 Finish with a few small stitches over and over on the back of the fabric and trim the thread.

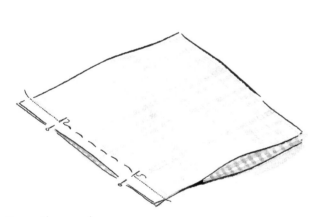

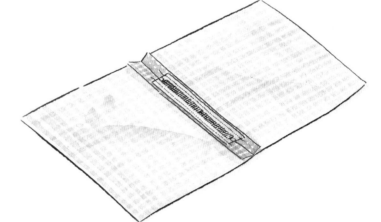

Inserting a zipper

1 With right sides together, pin the two fabric pieces together along the seam allowance. Measure the length of the zipper and mark a space centrally on the fabric to this measurement. Stitch from either end of the fabric to the mark for the opening. Baste the open section of the fabric and press the seam open.

2 Lay the closed zipper right side down along the basted area on the wrong side of the fabric, and baste in place. Using the zipper foot on your machine, topstitch the zip in place on the right side of the fabric, evenly down both sides and across both ends. Remove the basting stitches and open the zipper.

Kitchen AND Laundry

Kitchen curtain

This lightweight patchwork curtain is quick to make and will transform a kitchen or utility room. Large squares of pretty floral fabrics have been teamed with crisp ticking and a solid-colored fabric to break up the pattern. A length of curtain wire threaded through a channel across the top makes it simple to hang in place and take down to launder.

MATERIALS
Assorted fabrics to cut into 12-in. (30-cm) squares

Sewing thread to match fabrics

Curtain wire and eyelets

2 hooks

EQUIPMENT
Pencil, paper, and scissors for pattern

Tape measure

Pins

Fabric scissors

Sewing machine

Iron

SEAMS
Take ½-in. (1-cm) seam allowances throughout unless otherwise stated

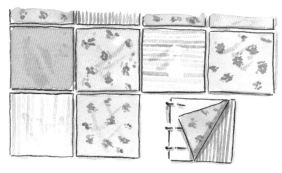

1 Measure and cut out a 12-in. (30-cm) square of paper. Pin onto the fabrics and cut out squares. Arrange the squares so that no two squares of the same fabric are next to each other, using enough squares to create a panel of the size that you need for your curtain. With right sides together, pin and stitch the squares together, working in horizontal lines.

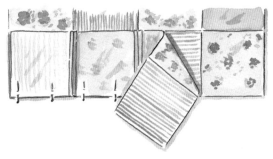

2 Press the seams open. With right sides together, pin and stitch the strips together in the correct order and again press the seams open.

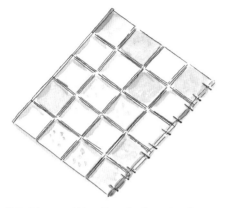

3 Fold over ⅜in. (1cm) along both vertical sides and fold this over again by ¾in. (2cm). Pin and stitch in place.

4 Fold the top edge and bottom edge over to the wrong side by ⅜in. (1cm) and again by 1¼in. (3cm). Stitch along the inside edge of the folded part to make a channel at the top, and a hem at the bottom. Press the curtain. Fix the hooks below the work surface, one on each side of the opening. Thread curtain wire with an eyelet at each end through the top channel, then hang in place by attaching the eyelets to the hooks.

Pan holder

This practical pan holder is very straightforward to make and requires only limited sewing skills. Choose a boldly patterned fabric for a striking look and line with thick batting (wadding) to provide adequate protection from the heat. Hang it up by the fabric loop and it will always be on hand when you need it.

Skills needed:

- **Machine sewing seams**
- **Trimming corners**
- **Slipstitching**

MATERIALS
40in. (1m) of patterned fabric
10in. (25cm) of solid-colored fabric
Sewing thread to match fabrics
20in. (50cm) of thick batting (wadding)

EQUIPMENT
Tape measure
Fabric scissors
Pins
Sewing machine
Masking tape
Sewing needle

SEAMS
Take ⅝-in. (1.5-cm) seam allowances throughout unless otherwise stated.

1 Cut a 7 x 10-in. (18 x 25-cm) piece of patterned fabric and two 2½ x 10-in. (6.5 x 25-cm) pieces of solid-colored fabric. With right sides together, lay each solid-colored piece along one long side of the patterned piece. Pin and machine stitch together. Press the seams open.

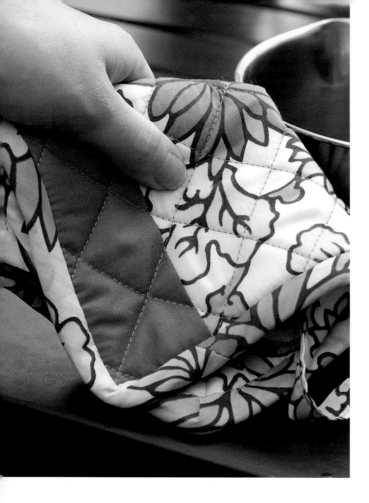

2 Cut two 10¼-in. (26-cm) squares of thick batting (wadding). Place the backing fabric wrong side up on your work surface, with the batting (wadding) squares on top and the front of the cover right side up on top of the batting (wadding). Pin all layers together. Stick a piece of masking tape diagonally from one corner to the other, and machine stitch along the edge of the tape. Reposition the tape 1¼in. (3cm) from the stitching line. Stitch along the edge. Continue until you reach the corner. Lay masking tape across the other two corners and repeat the stitching process until the whole mat is quilted.

3 Cut a piece of fabric on the bias 40in. (1m) long and 1½in. (4cm) wide (join several pieces together if necessary). With right sides together, pin it all around the right side of the mat, aligning the raw edges. Fold under the end for a neat finish, and machine stitch in place. Trim the corners.

4 To make the hanging loop, cut a 7 x 2-in. (18 x 5-cm) strip of patterned fabric. Fold over the long edges by ⅜in. (1cm) and then fold in half lengthwise. Machine stitch, stitching as close to the edge as possible. Fold the bias strip over to the back of the mat and turn under ⅜in. (1cm). Pin, then slipstitch to the mat all the way around, centering the loop on one side.

cook's apron

Sure to have you reaching for your baking tools, this cute apron is made from strip patchwork and has a real vintage feel. Strips of two different fabrics of equal width are alternated to form the "skirt" and embellished with rickrack in a complementary color. Add a patchwork pocket to make it practical as well as pretty, if you like.

Skills needed:

- **Machine sewing seams**
- **Trimming corners**
- **Running stitch or machine gathering**
- **Topstitching**

MATERIALS

8in. (20cm) of 54-in. (137-cm) wide patterned fabric

12in. (30cm) of 54-in. (137-cm) wide spotty fabric

30in. (75cm) of 54-in. (137-cm) wide gingham fabric

99in. (2.5m) of rickrack braid

Sewing thread to match fabrics

EQUIPMENT

Tape measure

Fabric scissors

Pins

Sewing machine

Iron

Sewing needle

SEAMS

Take ½-in. (1-cm) seam allowances throughout unless otherwise stated.

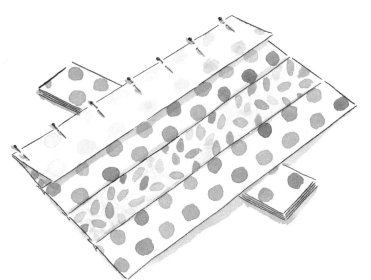

1 To make the apron, measure and cut strips of the patterned and spotty fabrics 3¾in. (9cm) wide by 21½in. (54cm) long. You will need five strips of spotty fabric and four strips of patterned fabric. With right sides together, pin and stitch the strips together alternating the fabrics but starting and ending with the spotty fabric. Press the seams open.

2 Cut lengths of rickrack 22in. (56cm) long and pin, then stitch them along one side of each of the patterned strips. Trim the ends neatly.

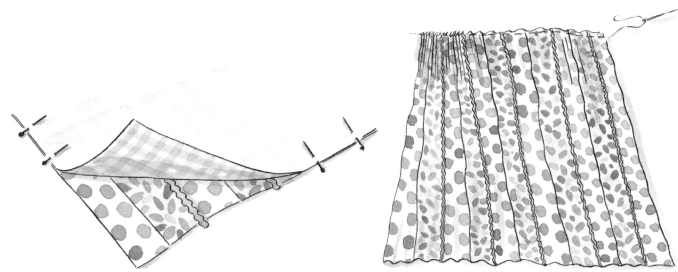

3 Cut a piece of gingham fabric 25¾ x 21½in. (65 x 54cm). With right sides together, pin, then stitch this to the patchwork piece, leaving an opening about 4in. (10cm) long at the center of the top of the apron. Snip the corners (see page 13) and turn the right way out through the opening. Press.

4 Make a running stitch or sew machine gathering (see page 11) across the top of the apron skirt and gather the fabric up to a width of about 18in. (45cm). Finish with a few stitches to secure the gathering.

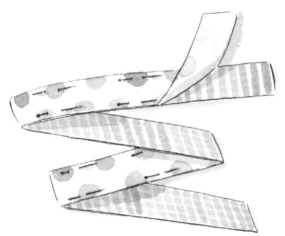

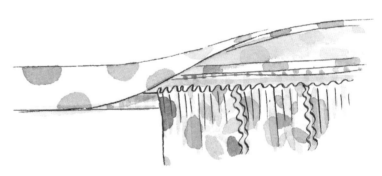

5 To make the waistband, measure and cut a strip of spotty fabric and a strip of gingham fabric 2½ x 54in. (6.5 x 137cm). You can join lengths together if the fabric width is narrower than 54in. (137cm). With right sides together, pin and stitch the strips together along both ends and one long side. Turn the right way out.

6 Press under ⅜in. (1cm) along the raw edges of both strips of fabric. Lay the gathered edge of the apron skirt inside the center of the waistband, placing it up from the edge by ⅜in. (1cm), and pin in place. Topstitch (see page 17) along the fold to hold the apron in place, continuing round all edges of the waistband. Press.

Tea cozy

Keep tea piping hot with this vintage-feel tea cozy. The combination of gingham and floral fabrics, edged with pretty braids, is a surefire winner. You could easily make a taller cozy to fit a coffee pot—or for a cute, homely feel, why not try making miniature versions from little scraps of fabric to cover your breakfast boiled eggs?

Skills needed:

- **Using templates**
- **Topstitching**
- **Machine sewing seams**
- **Slipstitching**

MATERIALS
20in. (50cm) of pink fabric

20in. (50cm) of gingham fabric

20in. (50cm) of floral fabric

30in. (75cm) of gingham ribbon

30in. (75cm) of floral trim

20in. (50cm) of medium-weight batting (wadding)

Sewing thread to match fabrics

EQUIPMENT
Paper, pencil, and scissors for pattern

Tape measure

Fabric scissors

Iron

Pins

Sewing machine

Sewing needle

SEAMS
Take ⅝-in. (1.5-cm) seam allowances throughout unless otherwise stated.

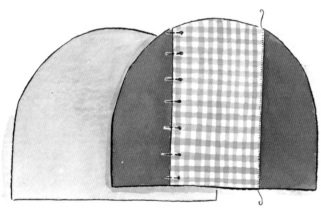

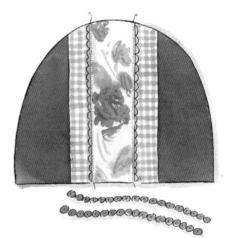

1 Using the template on page 91, make a pattern to cut two pieces of pink fabric. Cut a panel of gingham measuring 7¾ x 10¾in. (19.5 x 27cm). Fold over ⅜in. (1cm) to the wrong side along both long sides of the gingham and press. (Use the lines of the gingham as a guide, to get a straight edge.) Center the gingham panel on the front of one of the pink fabric pieces and machine stitch it in place. Trim off any excess gingham, following the curve of the pink fabric.

2 Cut a piece of floral fabric measuring 3 x 10¾in. (9 x 27cm) and fold under both long edges by ⅝in. (1.5cm). Pin the floral fabric centrally onto the gingham fabric, slipping a length of gingham ribbon under both edges. Machine stitch through all layers. Stitch a length of floral trim along both edges of the gingham fabric.

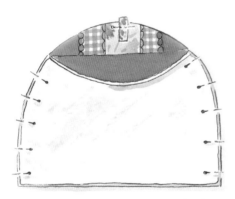

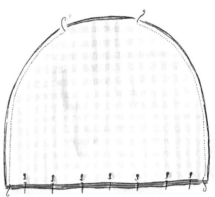

3 To make the hanging loop, cut a 1½ x 2-in. (3.5 x 5-cm) piece of floral fabric. Fold over each long side by ⅜in. (1cm), and then fold in half lengthwise and machine stitch along the folded edges and press. Using the pattern, cut two pieces of medium-weight batting (wadding). Lay one piece on your work surface, with the front of the tea cozy right side up on top, and pin the hanging loop to the center of the curved side. Lay the back of the tea cozy right side down on top, followed by a piece of batting (wadding). Machine stitch all around the curved edge.

4 Using the pattern, cut two pieces of gingham. Machine stitch around the curved side, leaving an 8-in. (20-cm) gap along the top. Put the gingham over the front of the tea cozy, right sides together. Stitch together around the bottom. Turn right side out and slipstitch the opening closed on the gingham fabric.

Ironing board cover

Even purely functional items such as ironing board covers don't have to be dull! Use a favorite fabric to make a padded cover that is held in place with a drawstring, making it easy to remove and wash. Thick cotton fabrics work best for this project, lined with cotton batting that will withstand some heat.

MATERIALS
30in. (75cm) of plain white cotton fabric

30in. (75cm) of patterned fabric

30in. (75cm) of lightweight cotton batting (wadding)

Approx. 79in. (2m) of white ribbon

Sewing thread to match fabrics

EQUIPMENT
Ironing board

Pencil or fabric marker

Tape measure

Fabric scissors

Pins

Sewing machine

Iron

Safety pin

SEAMS
Take ⅝-in. (1.5-cm) seam allowances throughout unless otherwise stated.

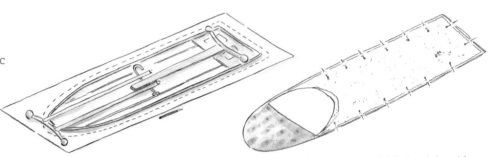

1 Lay the ironing board on the white fabric and draw around it, adding 4in. (10cm) all around. Cut out. Cut a piece of patterned fabric and a piece of cotton batting (wadding) to the same size.

2 Lay the patterned fabric right side up on your work surface. Place the white cotton on top, with the batting (wadding) on top of the cotton. Pin and machine stitch through all the layers, leaving an opening of about 6in. (15cm) at the straight end. Snip the seam allowance off at the corners, and trim the seam allowance to ¼in. (6mm) all the way around.

3 Turn the cover right side out, and press. Measure and machine stitch a line 2in. (5cm) in from the edge all the way around to make a channel, leaving a gap of 1in. (2.5cm) at the straight end.

4 Attach a safety pin to the end of the ribbon, and thread it through the gap, into the channel, and all the way around the cover, then out of the gap again. Pull the ribbon ends to gather the cover over the ironing board, and secure with a bow.

Peg bag

This charming bag is the perfect place to store wooden clothes pins and will brighten up any wash day. It's made in a vintage-style floral fabric topped off with a coordinating ribbon and rickrack braid, with a bright gingham lining just visible around the opening. A child's wooden hanger is the perfect size to use inside the bag, so that you can hang it on a hook in the kitchen or utility room when not in use—or on the washing line when you are hanging out the laundry.

MATERIALS
20in. (50cm) of floral fabric

20in. (50cm) of gingham fabric

20in. (50cm) of pink grosgrain ribbon, ³⁄₈in. (1cm) wide

20in. (50cm) of blue rickrack braid

Sewing thread to match fabrics

Coat hanger

EQUIPMENT
Pencil, paper, and scissors for pattern

Fabric scissors

Pins

Sewing machine

Iron

Sewing needle

SEAMS
Take ⅝-in. (1.5-cm) seam allowances throughout unless otherwise stated.

1 Enlarge the templates on page 92 by 200% to make paper patterns. Cut one back piece, and one top and one bottom front piece from the floral fabric. Repeat using the gingham fabric. With right sides together, pin and then machine stitch the floral and gingham top pieces together along the curve. Trim the seam allowance, turn right side out, and press.

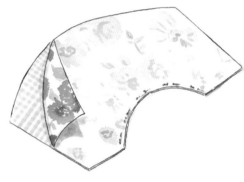

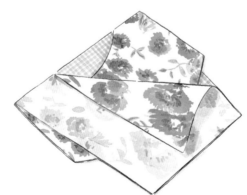

2 Lay the gingham bottom front piece right side up on your work surface. Place the top front piece right side up on top of it and the floral bottom front piece wrong side up on top of that. Machine stitch along the top edge, stitching through all layers.

3 Turn right side out and press. Pin a length of blue rickrack braid across the bag about ⅝in. (1.5cm) from the top of the base, with a length of pink grosgrain ribbon about ⅜in. (1cm) below that, and machine stitch in place.

4 Lay the front of the bag right side up on your work surface, with the floral back piece right side down on top of it. Place the gingham back piece right side up on top. Machine stitch all around the edge, leaving a gap of about ¾in. (2cm) in the center top. Turn right side out. Insert the coat hanger, and handstitch a grosgrain ribbon bow below the hook.

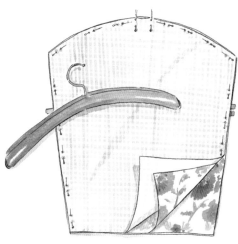

CHAPTER 2

Living
AND Dining

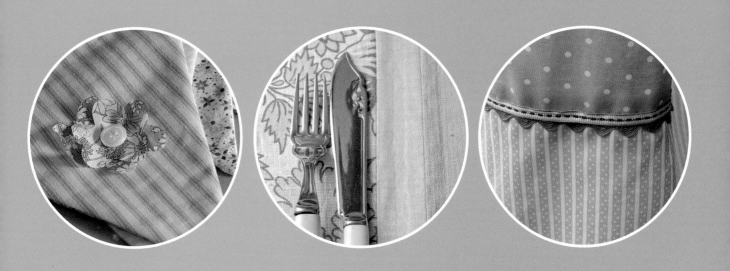

Floral throw pillow

Add a pretty, country feel to your couch with these lovely floral throw pillows. These use the same fabric throughout, but you could choose a coordinating fabric for the back, so that you can turn the pillow over and change the look to suit your mood. The covers are very easy to make, as they have no zippers or buttons but are fastened with neat little fabric ties. To make them even simpler, you could replace the ties with ribbon.

Skills needed:

● **Making ties**   ● **Machine sewing seams**

MATERIALS (PER PILLOW)
30in. (75cm) of floral fabric

Sewing thread to match fabric

18-in. (45-cm) square pillow form

EQUIPMENT
Tape measure

Fabric scissors

Pins

Sewing machine

MEASUREMENTS
18-in. (45-cm) square

SEAMS
Take ⅝-in. (1.5-cm) seam allowances throughout unless otherwise stated.

1 Cut a piece of fabric measuring 19 x 19¼in. (48 x 49cm). Along one short edge, fold over ⅜in. (1cm) and then another ⅝in. (1.5cm) to the wrong side. Machine stitch in place.

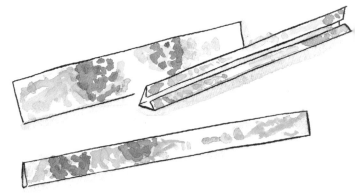

2 Cut four 3 x 10-in. (7 x 25-cm) strips of fabric. Fold each one in half, wrong sides together, and press. Open out. Along both long sides, fold over ⅝in. (1.5cm) to the wrong side and press. At one short end, fold over ⅝in. (1.5cm) and press.

3 Fold the whole strip in half along the center fold line. Machine stitch along the strip, stitching as close to the unfolded edge as possible, and across the folded end. Press.

4 Cut a 19 x 7½-in. (48 x 19-cm) rectangle of fabric. Along one long edge, fold over ⅜in. (1cm) and then another ⅝in. (1.5cm) to the wrong side. Pin and machine stitch.

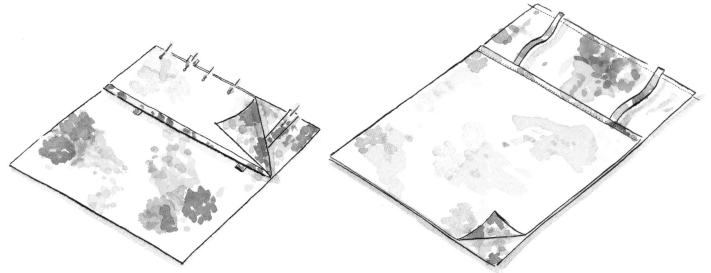

5 Cut a 19-in. (48-cm) square of fabric. With right sides together, pin the raw edge of the rectangle from Step 4 to one side of the square, inserting the open end of one tie into the seam 4½in. (12cm) from one corner and another one 4½in. (12cm) from the other corner. Machine stitch in place. Press the seam open.

6 Lay this piece wrong side down on your work surface. With right sides together, place the other piece of fabric from Step 1 on top, aligning the hemmed side with the seam on the bottom piece.

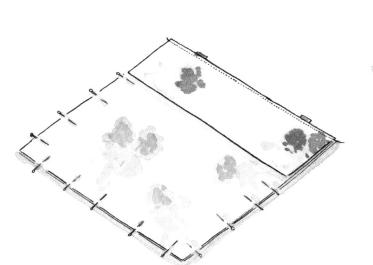

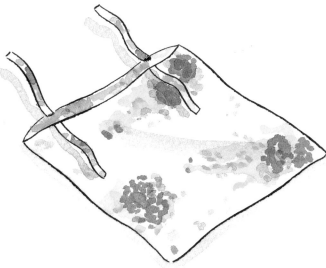

7 Fold the flap over the top, then pin and machine stitch around the three sides of the square. Turn the cover right side out.

8 Take the remaining two ties, fold under ⅝in. (1.5cm) at the raw ends and machine stitch them onto the pillow cover, aligning them with the ties already in place. Press the cover. Insert the pillow form and tie the ties in a neat bow to close.

Dotty patchwork pillow

Stitch large circles of patterned fabric onto plain linen to make this delightfully dotty pillow cover. Choose scraps of your favorite fabrics for the dots and edge them with a small zigzag stitch to prevent them from fraying.

Skills needed:

- **Using a pattern**
- **Machine zigzag stitch**
- **Machine sewing seams**
- **Inserting a zipper**
- **Trimming corners**

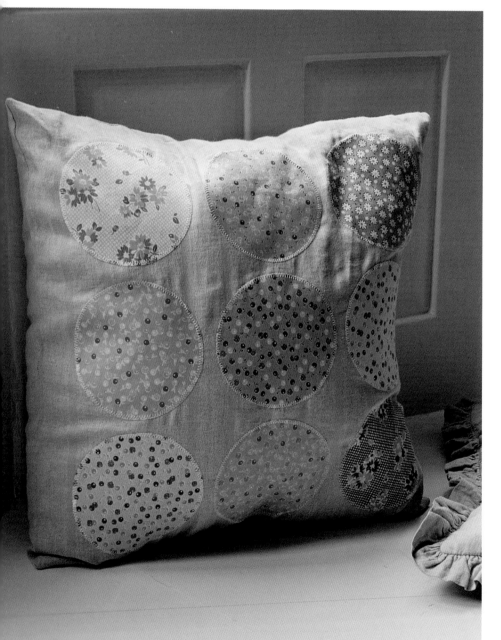

MATERIALS

10in. (25cm) each of a selection of patterned fabrics

20in. (50cm) of natural-colored linen

Sewing thread to match fabrics

14-in. (35-cm) zipper

18-in. (45-cm) square pillow form

EQUIPMENT

Compass, pencil, paper, and scissors for pattern

Tape measure

Pins

Fabric scissors

Sewing machine

Iron

MEASUREMENTS

18-in. (45-cm) square

SEAMS

Take ⅝-in. (1.5-cm) seam allowances throughout unless otherwise stated.

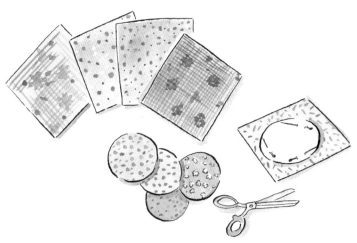

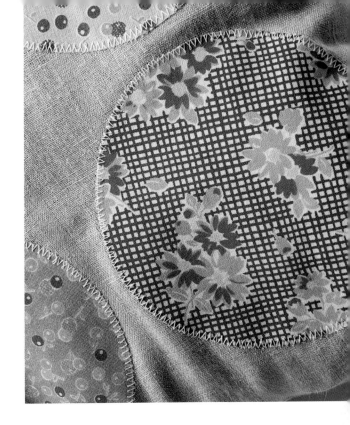

1 Using a compass, draw a circle 5in. (13cm) in diameter on paper. Cut out and use as a paper pattern. Pin to the fabrics and cut out nine fabric circles.

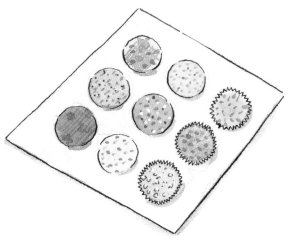

2 Cut two 19-in. (48-cm) squares of linen. Lay one piece right side up on your work surface and arrange the fabric circles on top, leaving ⅜in. (1cm) between each one and 1½in. (3.5cm) all the way around the edge. Using a small zigzag stitch on the sewing machine, stitch all around each fabric circle, staying as close to the edge as you can.

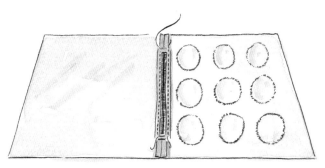

3 With right sides together, baste the two linen squares together along one side using the seam allowance. Machine stitch from each corner for 2in. (5cm). Press the seam open and lay the zipper right side down on the wrong side of the seam. Baste and then machine stitch the zipper in place (see page 15). Remove the basting stitches.

4 With right sides together, pin and machine stitch the remaining three sides of the fabric squares together. Snip the corners, open the zipper, and turn the pillow cover right side out. Press, then insert the pillow form.

Simple curtain with patterned border

Liven up a plain curtain with patterned borders and braids, or use this method to lengthen existing curtains to fit a new window. Choose fabrics with similar colors, mixing spots, stripes, and florals, and add rickrack braid and ribbon for extra decoration.

Skills needed:

- **Machine sewing seams**
- **Machine-stitched hems**

WORKING OUT FABRIC QUANTITIES
To work out the length of spotted fabric you will need, measure from the top of the curtain pole to where you want the bottom of the curtain to fall, then deduct 15¼ in. (39cm), and cut that amount of spotted fabric. To work out the width of the fabric you will need, allow for at least 1½ times the width of the curtain pole for a slightly gathered curtain. For a wider window, make two curtains if the fabric is not wide enough to allow for this.

MATERIALS
Spotted fabric
20in. (50cm) of striped fabric
20in. (50cm) of floral fabric
Sewing thread to match fabrics
2 lengths of braid
1 length of jumbo rickrack braid
Curtain lining fabric
Curtain heading tape

EQUIPMENT
Tape measure
Fabric scissors
Pins
Sewing machine
Iron

SEAMS
Take ⅝-in. (1.5-cm) seam allowances throughout unless otherwise stated.

1 Cut a piece of spotted fabric to the required size. Cut a piece of striped fabric 10¼in. (26cm) deep and a piece of floral fabric 11½in. (29cm) deep; both pieces should be the same width as the spotted fabric. With right sides together, pin and machine stitch the striped fabric to the bottom of the spotted fabric and the floral fabric to the bottom of the striped fabric. Press open the seams.

2 Pin and machine stitch one piece of braid over the join between the floral and striped fabrics. Pin and stitch the rickrack braid along the join between the striped and spotted fabrics. Lay the second piece of braid over half of the rickrack, and stitch in place.

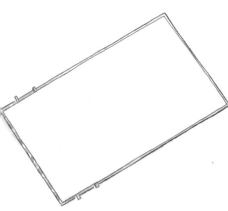

3 Cut a piece of lining fabric the same length as the curtain and 1¼in. (3cm) narrower. With right sides together, pin and machine stitch the lining fabric to the curtain along both long sides. Turn right side out and press.

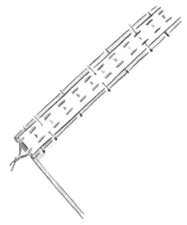

4 At the top of the curtain, turn over ⅜in. (1cm) to the wrong side. Turn over an additional 2in. (5cm) and pin. Cut the curtain tape to be 1in. (2.5cm) wider than the curtain on each side. Pin the curtain heading tape along this folded section, tucking the ends of the tape inside the folds at either end. Machine stitch close to the top, bottom, and side edges of the tape to hold it in place, taking care not to sew over the threads of the tape. Hem the bottom of the curtain by folding over ⅜in. (1cm) and another 1¼in. (3cm) and machine stitch in place.

Throw pillow with ribbon stripes

Skills needed:

- **Topstitching**
- **Machine-stitching buttonholes**
- **Machine sewing seams**
- **Trimming corners**
- **Sewing on buttons**

This is the perfect way to use up all those leftover bits of ribbon that never seem to be quite long enough to be useful. Collect together ribbons and braids in similar colors and stitch them onto solid-colored fabric to make a stylish pillow cover that no one would guess was made from scraps.

MATERIALS
20in. (50cm) of solid-colored fabric

Sewing thread to match fabrics and ribbons

Selection of ribbons in toning colors and various widths

13¾ x 20-in. (35 x 50-cm) pillow form

3 buttons

EQUIPMENT
Tape measure

Fabric scissors

Pins

Sewing machine

Iron

Sewing needle

MEASUREMENTS
13¾ x 20-in. (35 x 50-cm)

SEAMS
Take ⅝-in. (1.5-cm) seam allowances throughout unless otherwise stated.

1 Cut two 15¾ x 15¼-in. (40 x 39-cm) rectangles of solid-colored fabric. Fold over and press ⅜in. (1cm) to the wrong side along one 15¾-in. (40-cm) edge of each piece. Fold over another ⅝in. (1.5cm) on one piece and 2in. (5cm) on the other and topstitch close to the edge.

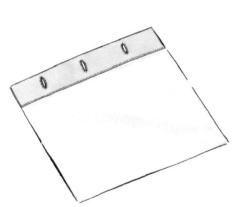

2 Make three buttonholes along this wider border (see page 11) to fit the size of the buttons you are using.

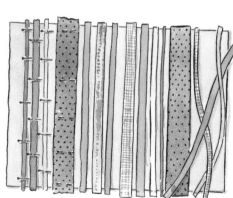

3 Cut a 15 x 21-in. (38 x 53-cm) rectangle of solid-colored fabric. Lay it on your work surface and place the ribbons on it until you are happy with the arrangement. Pin them in place, then baste and machine stitch each one onto the fabric.

4 Lay the ribbon-covered piece right side up on your work surface, with the buttonholed back piece right side down on top, aligning the raw edges. Place the other back piece right side down on top, again aligning the raw edges, and pin in place. Machine stitch around the edges, trim the corners to reduce bulk, and turn right side out. Sew three buttons onto the back in the required position. Press and then insert the pillow form.

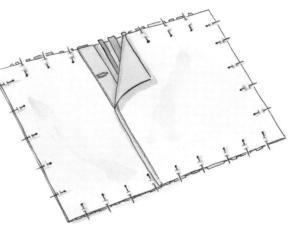

Place mat and napkin

Add a touch of elegance to your dinner table with these smart place mats and matching napkins. Quick and easy to make, they would be an ideal wedding or housewarming gift that the recipients will treasure for many years to come. As table linen requires regular laundering, make sure you wash all the fabrics before you start sewing so that there's no risk of them shrinking once the project is finished.

Skills needed:

- **Machine sewing seams**
- **Trimming corners**
- **Slipstitching**
- **Topstitching**

MATERIALS

For each place mat:

20in. (50cm) of solid-colored fabric

20in. (50cm) of patterned fabric

20in. (50cm) of gingham fabric

20in. (50cm) of medium-weight iron-on interfacing

For each napkin:

20in. (50cm) of patterned fabric

20in. (50cm) of gingham fabric

Sewing thread to match fabrics

EQUIPMENT

Tape measure

Fabric scissors

Pins

Sewing machine

Iron

Sewing needle

SEAMS

Take ⅝-in. (1.5-cm) seam allowances throughout unless otherwise stated.

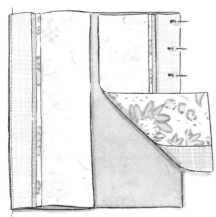

1 For each place mat, cut a 13½ x 10-in. (34 x 26-cm) rectangle of solid-colored fabric, two 13½ x 4½-in. (34 x 12-cm) rectangles of patterned fabric and two 13½ x 2 ¼-in. (34 x 6-cm) rectangles of gingham fabric. With right sides together, machine stitch one gingham piece along each long side of the solid-colored fabric, then machine stitch one patterned piece to the other long side of each gingham piece. Press the seams open.

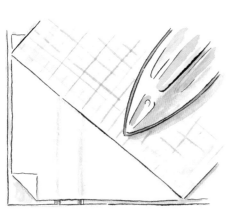

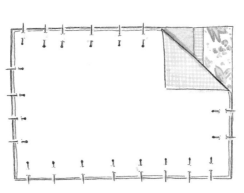

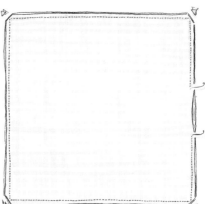

2 Cut a 13½ x 19½-in. (34 x 50-cm) piece of interfacing. Lay the interfacing on the wrong side of the fabric panel, with the rough side down. Place a damp cloth on top and iron with a medium iron to fuse the interfacing to the fabric.

3 For the backing, cut a piece of gingham and a piece of interfacing, each measuring 13½ x 19½in. (34 x 50cm). Iron the interfacing to the reverse of the gingham, as before. Lay the front of the mat right side up on your work surface with the back piece on top, right side down. Machine stitch all around the edge, leaving a gap of about 4in. (10cm) in one side. Trim the corners. Turn right side out and slipstitch the opening closed. Press and then topstitch all around the edges.

4 For each napkin, cut a 16-in. (40-cm) square of patterned fabric and a 16-in. (40-cm) square of gingham fabric. With right sides together, machine stitch all around, leaving a gap of about 4in. (10cm) in one side. Snip across the corners. Turn right side out and slipstitch the opening closed. Press and then topstitch all around the edges, 1in. (2.5cm) from the edge.

Quilted coasters

Protect your tabletop with these cute coasters, which are the perfect project to get you into quilting. Squares of fabric are joined to make one large square, which is then backed and machine quilted. What could be easier? Use a lighter weight batting (wadding) so that the coasters lie flat.

Skills needed:

- **Using a pattern**
- **Machine sewing seams**
- **Trimming corners**
- **Slipstitching**
- **Topstitching**

MATERIALS

18 x 12in. (45 x 30cm) each of 2 different design fabrics

Sewing thread to match fabrics

10 x 10in. (28 x 28cm) of fabric in a coordinating design

10 x 10in. (28 x 28cm) of batting (wadding)

EQUIPMENT

Paper, pencil, and scissors for pattern

Tape measure

Fabric scissors

Pins

Sewing machine

Iron

Sewing needle

SEAMS

Take ½-in. (1-cm) seam allowances throughout unless otherwise stated.

1 Draw a square on paper measuring 3in. (8cm) on each side and cut out to use as a pattern. Using the pattern, cut out two squares each of two different fabrics. With right sides together, pin and stitch two of the squares (one of each fabric) together. Press the seams open.

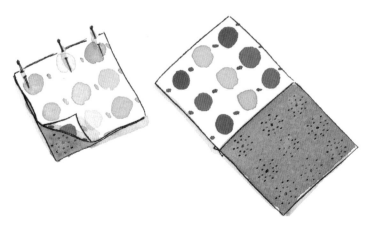

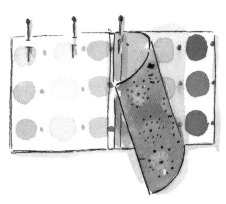

2 With right sides together, pin and stitch the two strips together, ensuring that squares of different fabrics are next to each other in a checkerboard design. Again, press the seam open.

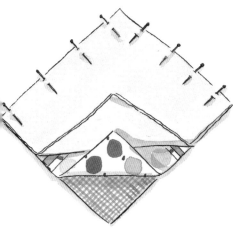

3 Cut a square of the third fabric measuring 5in. (14cm) square and cut a piece of batting (wadding) to this size. Lay the backing square right side up on the work surface with the patchwork square right side down on top of it. Place the batting (wadding) square on top of this. Pin and stitch through all layers all the way round, leaving an opening of about ½in. (1cm) along one side.

4 Snip the corners and turn the right way out. Slipstitch the opening closed and press. Measure ½in. (1cm) in from the edge of the coaster and mark with pins. Topstitch along this line. Measure and mark at equal intervals from this line and topstitch in the same way to quilt the coaster. Repeat steps 1 to 4 to make three more coasters.

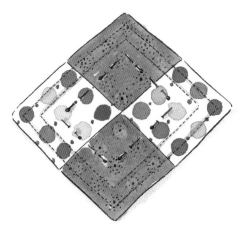

Mattress pillow for garden bench

This generously padded pillow transforms a hard garden chair or bench into a comfy corner in which to relax. The pretty felt tufts add a decorative touch and also hold all the layers of the pillow together.

Skills needed:

- **Machine sewing seams**
- **Box stitching**
- **Trimming corners**
- **Slipstitching**

ADJUSTING THE SIZES TO FIT YOUR BENCH
The instructions given here are for a pillow that is 20in. (50cm) square. If you need to adjust the measurements to fit your bench, remember to add 1¼in. (3cm) to the squares that you cut in Step 1 to allow for the seams. Similarly, the side strip needs to be 1¼in. (3cm) longer than the sum of the four sides—although the depth will remain the same.

MATERIALS
40in. (1m) of striped fabric

49in. (125cm) of thick batting (wadding)

10in. (25cm) of felt in 2 colors

Sewing thread to match fabrics

Embroidery floss

EQUIPMENT
Tape measure

Fabric scissors

Sewing machine

Iron

Pins

Sewing needle

Pinking shears

Long needle

MEASUREMENTS
20in. (50cm) square

SEAMS
Take ⅝-in. (1.5-cm) seam allowances throughout unless otherwise stated.

1 Cut two 21-in. (53-cm) squares of striped fabric.

2 Cut two strips of fabric 5½in. (14cm) long by the width of the fabric. Cut off the selvages. With right sides together, machine stitch the two strips together. Press the seam open. Cut the strip to 80in. (203cm) long.

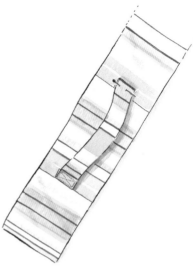

3 To make the handle, cut a 9 x 3½-in. (24 x 9-cm) strip of fabric. Fold in half lengthwise, with right sides together, and machine stitch down the long raw edge. Turn right side out and press so that the seam runs down the center. Turn the ends under to the wrong side by ⅝in. (1.5cm), and press.

4 Pin the handle onto the long fabric strip with one end 6½in. (15.5cm) from one end and the other end 7½in. (19cm) from that. Machine stitch a square around each end of the strip and then a cross from corner to corner of the stitched squares (see page 12).

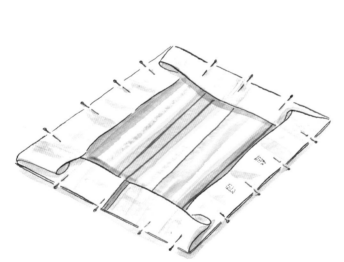

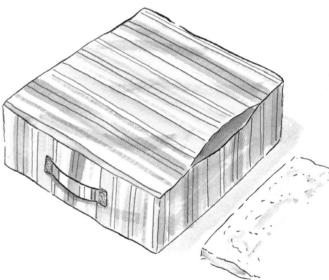

5 With right sides together, pin and machine stitch the short ends of the long strip together. Press the seam open. With right sides together, pin and machine stitch the side panel to one of the squares, placing the seam of the side panel at a corner. Snip the corners of the square and press.

6 Pin and stitch the other side of the side panel to the remaining square, leaving an opening of about 8in. (20cm) in one side, and turn right side out. Cut four 20-in. (50-cm) squares of batting (wadding). Push them through the opening, making sure that the corners of the batting (wadding) are pushed right into the corners of the cover. Slipstitch the opening closed.

7 Using pinking shears, cut four 2½-in. (6-cm) circles from one color of felt and four 1½-in. (4-cm) circles from the second color of felt.

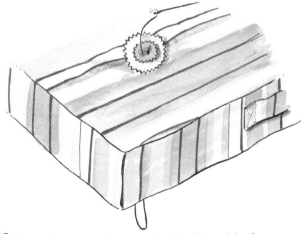

8 At each corner, place a pin 6in. (16cm) in from each side to mark the positions for the felt circles. Thread a long needle with embroidery floss and tie a knot about 1½in. (4cm) from the end. Thread the needle through the center of a small felt circle and then through a larger felt circle and push the needle through the pillow at the marked place. Pull the needle through the pillow.

9 Stitch back up from the back of the pillow to the front through the felt circles. Repeat to secure. Pull the embroidery floss to gather the pillow and tie a knot to secure it. Trim the ends of the thread to about 1¼in. (3cm). Repeat at the other corners.

Pretty bunting

When making sewing projects, there are inevitably lots of leftover pieces of fabric. Bunting is a quick and easy way of using up these scraps to create a cute decoration for just about anywhere in the home. Mix colors and patterns using different fabrics on each side of each triangle, finishing the bunting with simple flower and button embellishments and stitching them onto ribbon.

Skills needed:

- **Using templates and patterns**
- **Machine sewing seams**
- **Trimming seams**
- **Hand sewing**
- **Sewing on buttons**

MATERIALS
Scraps of fabrics at least 10 x 11in. (25 x 27cm)

Sewing thread to match fabrics

Ribbon

Buttons

EQUIPMENT
Paper, pencil, and scissors for pattern

Fabric scissors

Pins

Sewing machine

Iron

Sewing needle

SEAMS
Take ½-in. (1-cm) seam allowances throughout unless otherwise stated.

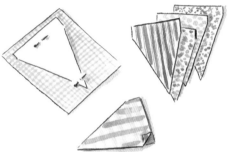

1 Using the template on page 93, cut out a paper pattern. Decide how many bunting triangles you would like and cut two fabric triangles for each one. With right sides together, pin and stitch two fabric triangles together, starting and finishing the stitches ⅞in. (2cm) from the top edge, leaving the top edge open.

2 Trim the seam allowance and turn the triangles the right way out. Press. Turn in ⅜in. (1cm) to the wrong side along both top edges of each triangle.

3 Slip the ribbon between the top opening of the triangles, and pin and stitch in place with a double row of stitches.

4 Using the templates on page 93, cut out a large and a small flower shape from paper and use them to cut out a large and small fabric flower for each triangle. Hand stitch the flowers onto the triangles, sewing a button in the middle of each.

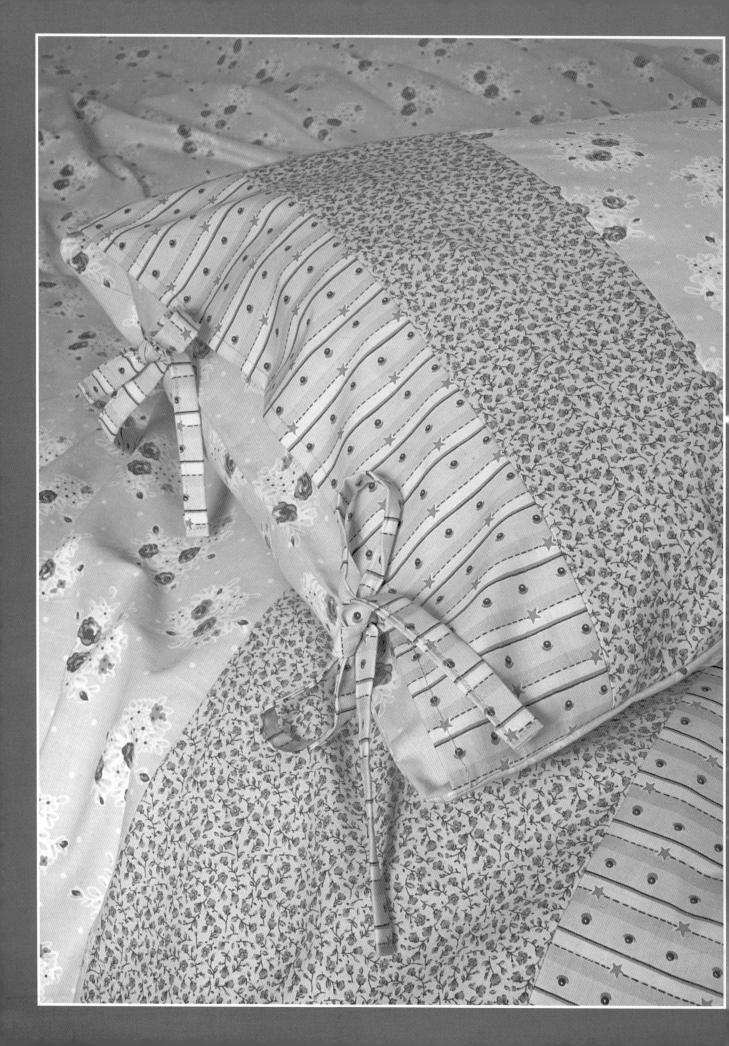

CHAPTER 3

Bedrooms

Flower-and-leaf lampshade

Skills needed:

- **Using a pattern**
- **Running stitch**
- **Sewing on buttons**

This is a great way of livening up a plain lampshade. Make fabric yo-yos, also known as Suffolk puffs, into sweet little flowers by stitching a button to the center and then simply glue them onto the shade with fabric leaf shapes to finish.

MATERIALS
10in. (25cm) each of 4 fabrics in pastel colors for the rosettes

Sewing thread to match fabrics

Selection of buttons

10in. (25cm) of green fabric for the leaf shapes

Round lampshade

Enough pompom fringe to go around the bottom of the shade plus ⅜in. (1cm)

Enough ¼-in. (5-mm) ribbon to go round the top of the shade plus ⅜in. (1cm)

EQUIPMENT
Compass, pencil, and paper for pattern

Tape measure

Pins

Fabric scissors

Sewing needle

Fast-drying craft glue

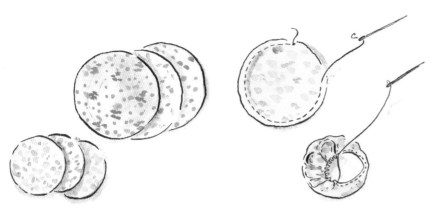

1 Using a compass, draw a 3½-in. (9-cm) circle and a 2½-in. (6-cm) circle on paper. Cut out the circles to use as patterns, then pin them onto your chosen fabrics and cut out the required number of each fabric in each size. Using a needle and thread, work a line of running stitch all around the edge of each circle, securing the thread at the beginning with a few small stitches. Pull the thread to gather the circle into a rosette.

2 Finish with a few small stitches to hold the rosette in place. Stitch a button to the center of each rosette. Draw a leaf shape on paper, and cut out. Pin the leaf pattern to green fabric. Cut out one or two leaves for each flower.

3 Using fast-drying craft glue, stick pompom fringe all around the bottom of the shade, overlapping the ends slightly. Make sure that the fringe is straight before the glue dries. Starting and finishing at the same side of the shade as the pompom fringe, glue ribbon around the top of the shade.

4 Glue the fabric rosettes onto the shade, holding them in place for a few seconds until they are firmly stuck. Apply a thin layer of glue to the back of the leaf shapes and glue them onto the shade, one or two per rosette.

Sheer curtain with ribbons

With so many lovely patterned sheer fabrics in the stores now, it is easy to make something practical that still makes a statement in a room. Here, I've used lengths of ribbons and braids to make a pretty border.

· ·

Skills needed:

● **Machine sewing seams**

● **Making a hem**

MATERIALS

Sheer fabric

5 different ribbons and rickrack braid, each the width of the finished curtain plus 4in. (10cm)

Sewing thread to match fabric

EQUIPMENT

Tape measure

Fabric scissors

Pins

Sewing machine

Iron

Sewing needle

WORKING OUT FABRIC QUANTITIES

If the curtain is to be pulled taut on the pole, you will need to cut a piece of fabric that is 2in. (5cm) wider and 2in. (5cm) longer than the window. If you want the curtain to be slightly gathered, allow about 25% extra when calculating the width.

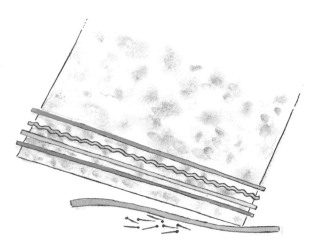

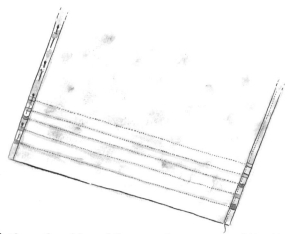

1 Cut a piece of sheer fabric to the required size (see box, above right). Arrange the ribbons and rickrack braid across the bottom of the fabric, leaving at least 1½in. (4cm) below the first ribbon to allow for the hem. Pin, baste, and machine stitch the ribbons and braid in place, and then trim the ends level with the edge of the fabric.

2 Along the sides of the curtain, turn over ⅜in. (1cm) and then another ⅝in. (1.5cm) to the wrong side and press. Pin and machine stitch in place.

3 Work out how many ties you will need: the first and last ties should be positioned about 1¼in. (3cm) from each side of the curtain and the remainder should be spaced about 6½in. (16cm) apart. For each pair of ties, cut a 17 x 5-in. (43 x 13-cm) piece of fabric. With right sides together, fold each piece of fabric in half and machine stitch along the length and across one short end. Turn right side out, press the raw end under by ⅝in. (1.5cm), and hand stitch closed. Fold the ties in half and pin to the top of the right side of the curtain. Cut a piece of fabric the same width as the curtain and 3in. (8cm) deep for the facing. With right sides together, pin it along the top of the curtain. Machine stitch in place.

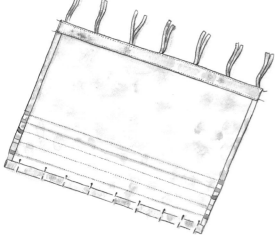

4 Fold the facing over to the wrong side of the curtain, and press ⅝in. (1.5cm) under along the remaining raw edges. Machine stitch the facing to the back of the curtain. At the bottom of the curtain, turn under ⅜in. (1cm), and then another ⅝in. (1.5cm) and machine stitch in place. Press.

Reversible duvet cover

Choose bold, contemporary fabrics for this reversible duvet cover. It can be difficult to buy fabric that is wide enough to fit a double bed, especially if you're using a fabric with a large pattern, so joining squares of fabric together is the perfect solution. The backing is made from two lengths of fabric stitched together to make the required width.

Skills needed:

● **Machine sewing seams** ● **Making a hem** ● **Trimming corners**

MATERIALS
90in. (225cm) each of 2 coordinating patterned fabrics

180in. (450cm) of striped fabric

Sewing thread to match fabrics

EQUIPMENT
Tape measure

Fabric scissors

Pins

Sewing machine

Iron

Tailor's chalk

MEASUREMENTS
78¾ x 78¾in. (200 x 200cm), to fit a standard double-bed duvet.

SEAMS
Take ½-in. (1-cm) seam allowances throughout unless otherwise stated.

 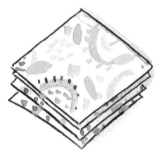

1 Cut eight 20¾-in. (53-cm) squares of each of the two patterned fabrics.

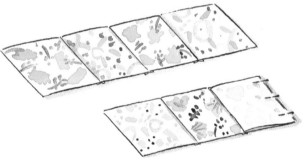

2 With right sides together, alternating the fabrics, pin and machine stitch the squares together to form four rows of four squares each. Press the seams open.

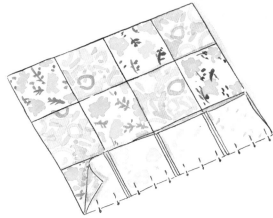

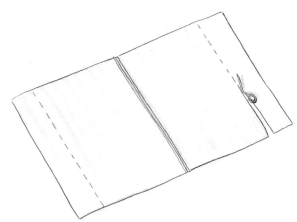

3 With right sides together, pin and machine stitch the four patchwork rows together to make a block of 16 squares. Press the seams open.

4 Cut two pieces of striped fabric 80in. (203cm) long and the full width of the fabric. Cut off one of the selvages on each piece. With right sides together, pin and machine stitch the pieces together along the cut edges. Press the seam open. Place the fabric on your work surface. Measure 40in. (101.5cm) either side of the center seam and use tailor's chalk to draw a line the full length of the fabric. Cut the fabric along these lines to a width of 80in. (203cm).

5 Measure 28in. (71.5cm) from one corner of the patchwork panel and make a cut ⅝in. (1.5cm) deep. Repeat from the other corner of the same edge of the panel. Press the central section to the wrong side by ¼in. (5mm) and then turn this over by another ⅜in. (1cm). Pin and machine stitch along the folded-over section. Repeat on the striped panel of fabric.

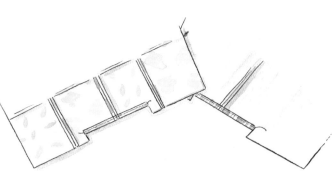

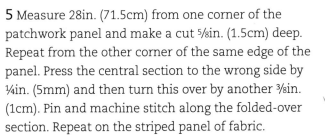

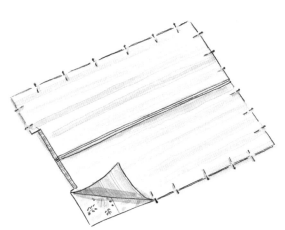

6 With right sides together, pin the front of the duvet cover to the back piece. Machine stitch from the stitched section at the bottom all the way around to the other end of the stitched section, using a seam allowance of ⅝in. (1.5cm).

7 Snip the corners of the seam allowance off, turn right side out, and press.

Roll-up shade

This simple shade, made from a bold floral fabric backed with a coordinating gingham check, can be made very quickly. As the shade has to be rolled up manually, it is ideal for rooms where it can be kept raised most of the time. Ribbons tied in pretty bows hold the shade in place when raised. The wooden dowelling in the bottom of the panel ensures that the shade forms a neat roll and does not sag.

MATERIALS

Patterned fabric

Coordinating gingham fabric

Sewing thread to match fabrics

Dowelling ½-in. (15mm) in diameter

2 metal rings 1½in. (4cm) in diameter

Length of 2 x 1-in. (5 x 2.5-cm) wood

Velcro (hook-and-loop tape)

Fast-drying craft glue

½-in. (12-mm) ribbon

EQUIPMENT

Tape measure

Fabric scissors

Pins

Sewing machine

Iron

Sewing needle

SEAMS

Take ⅝-in. (1.5-cm) seam allowances throughout unless otherwise stated.

MEASURING FOR SHADES

Decide whether you want the shade to fit inside the window frame or to align with the outside edges, then measure the distance for the finished width of the shade, and from top to bottom of the frame or the inner frame for the depth. Add the extra amounts as instructed in step 1, for seams, top, and bottom of the shade.

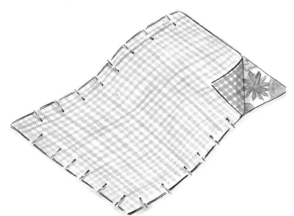

1 Cut a piece of patterned fabric and a piece of gingham fabric 1¼in. (3cm) wider and 2¾in. (7cm) longer than the finished shade. With right sides together, pin and machine stitch them together along both sides and the bottom. Snip off the corners.

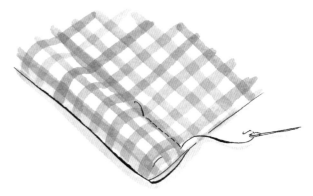

2 Turn right side out and press. Cut a piece of dowelling to fit the width of the panel and push it down inside the shade. Hand stitch just above the dowelling to keep it in place.

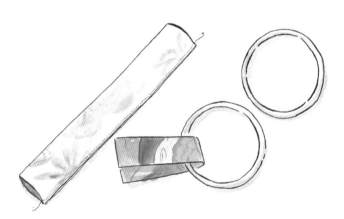

3 Make two tabs to hold the metal rings. Cut two 3½ x 9-in. (9 x 23-cm) rectangles of patterned fabric. With right sides together, fold them in half lengthways and machine stitch ⅝in. (1.5cm) from the edge. Turn right side out and press, with the seam in the middle of the tab. Thread each tab through a ring and fold in half.

4 Fold the open end of the shade over to the wrong side by ⅝in. (1.5cm) and again by 1½in. (4cm), placing the tabs under the hem 7in. (17cm) in from each side. Machine stitch along the bottom of the folded panel.

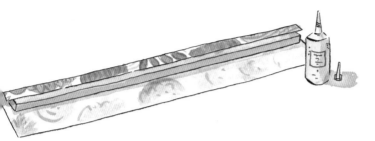

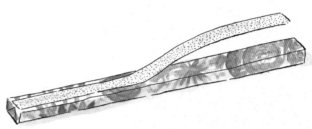

5 Cut a piece of wood the same width as the shade. Cut a piece of patterned fabric 5in. (13cm) deeper and 1½in. (4cm). wider than the wood. Center the wood on the fabric and glue it in place, folding the corners of the fabric in neatly.

6 Cut a piece of Velcro the same length as the wood and glue one half of it on to the wood. Screw the wood into the window frame, Velcro side facing away from the window.

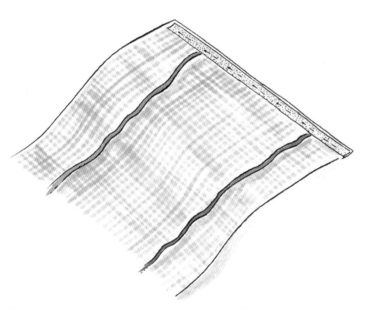

7 Cut two pieces of ribbon the same length as the shade. Pin and machine stitch the other half of the Velcro to the top of the shade on the wrong side, placing one length of ribbon 7in. (17cm) in from each side, under the Velcro.

8 Roll up the shade from the bottom and stick it onto the Velcroed wood. Cut two 10-in. (25-cm) lengths of ribbon and hand stitch one on to each ring. Bring the ribbon from the back of the shade to the front and tie to the shorter length of ribbon at the ring.

Little girl's duvet set

Skills needed:

- **Machine sewing seams**
- **Trimming corners**

Surprisingly simple to make, this pretty bed linen set will fit perfectly into any little princess's bedroom. Simply stitch two strips of co-ordinating fabric to either side of a panel of floral fabric to create a lovely patchwork effect. The key is to use small-print fabrics for the strips, to allow the bold floral design in the center to really make an impact.

MATERIALS

For the duvet cover:

30in. (75cm) each of 2 coordinating fabrics, 59in. (150cm) wide

50in. (125cm) of floral fabric, 59in. (150cm) wide

100in. (250cm) of backing fabric, 59in. (150cm) wide

For the pillow slip:

30in. (75cm) each of 2 coordinating fabrics, 59in. (150cm) wide

30in. (75cm) of floral fabric, 59in. (150cm) wide

30in. (75cm) of backing fabric, 59in. (150cm) wide

Sewing thread to match fabrics

EQUIPMENT

Tape measure

Fabric scissors

Pins

Sewing machine

Iron

MEASUREMENTS

53½ x 79in. (135 x 200cm) to fit a standard twin-bed (single-bed) duvet.

SEAMS

Take ⅝-in. (1.5-cm) seam allowances throughout unless otherwise stated.

TO MAKE DUVET COVER

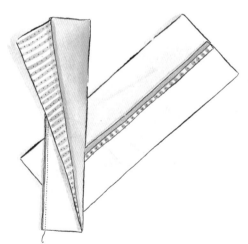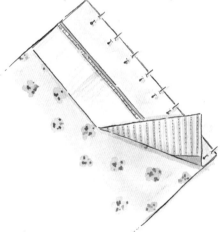

1 Cut two 10 x 54½-in. (25 x 138-cm) pieces of each of the coordinating border fabrics. With right sides together, pin and machine stitch one piece of each fabric together along one long side to make the border pieces. Press the seams open.

2 Cut a 43¾ x 54½-in. (111 x 138-cm) rectangle of floral fabric. With right sides together, pin and machine stitch one border piece to each end. Press the seams open.

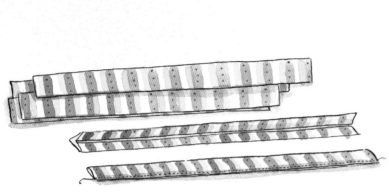

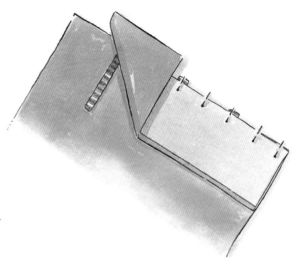

3 To make the ties, cut six 14 x 2-in. (36 x 5-cm) pieces of one of the coordinating fabrics. Along each long side of each tie, fold over ⅜in. (1cm) to the wrong side. Fold over ⅜in. (1cm) at one short end of each tie. Fold each tie in half lengthwise and stitch, stitching as close to the edge as possible.

4 Cut an 80 x 54½-in. (203 x 138-cm) rectangle of fabric for the back of the duvet cover. Pin three ties along one short end of the fabric on the right side, spacing them evenly. Cut a 15½ x 54½-in. (39 x 138-cm) strip of the backing fabric for the flap. Along one long edge, fold over ⅜in. (1cm) and then another ⅝in. (1.5cm) to the wrong side and machine stitch. With right sides together, aligning the raw edges, pin this strip on the backing fabric and machine stitch along the top, sandwiching the ties in between.

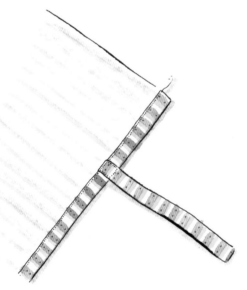

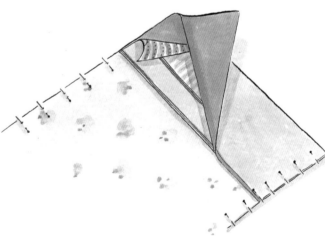

5 Along one short end of the front of the cover, fold over ⅝in. (1.5cm) and then another ⅝in. (1.5cm) to the wrong side. Place the raw ends of the remaining ties under the fold, spacing them as for the back piece, and machine stitch along the fold. Flip the ties over so that they hang off the bottom of the fabric and work a few stitches to keep them in place.

6 Lay the back piece on your work surface, right side up. Place the front piece on top, right side down, aligning the raw edges. Fold the flap on the back piece over the front piece. Pin and stitch along both long sides of the cover and the raw short side. Trim across the corners and turn right side out. Press.

TO MAKE THE PILLOW SLIP

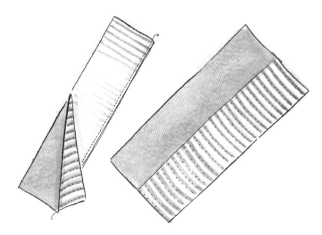

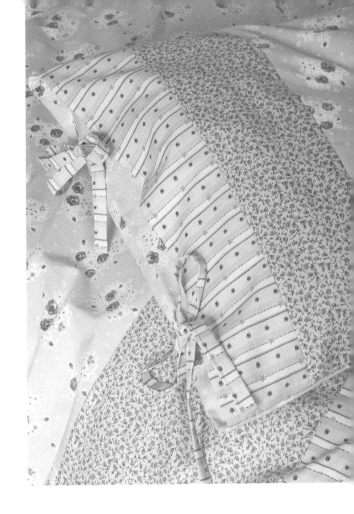

1 Cut two 20¾ x 4¾-in. (53 x 12-cm) rectangles of each of the coordinating border fabrics. With right sides together, pin and machine stitch one piece of each fabric together along one long side. Press the seams open. Cut a 16 x 20¾-in. (41 x 53-cm) rectangle of floral fabric. Pin and machine stitch one border piece to each long end. Press the seams open.

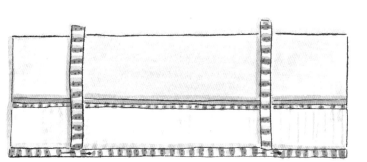

2 Make four ties, as in Step 3 of the duvet cover. Attach two ties to the front of the pillow slip, as in Step 5 of the duvet cover.

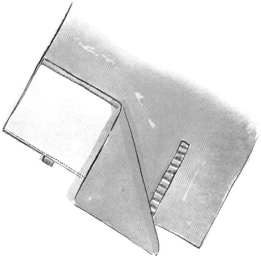

3 Cut a 30¾ x 20¾-in. (78 x 53-cm) piece of fabric for the back of the pillow slip and a 7½ x 20¾-in. (19 x 53-cm) piece for the flap. Hem one long side of the flap, as in Step 4 of the duvet cover. Lay the back piece right side up on your work surface. Place the two remaining ties on top, spacing them as for the front piece. Place the hemmed flap right side down on top, aligning the raw edges, and machine stitch. Follow Step 6 of the duvet cover to sew the pillow slip together.

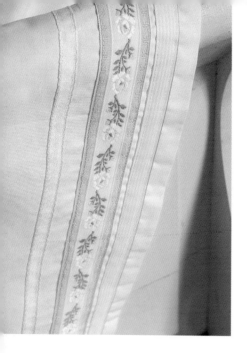

Sheet with ribbon trim

There is nothing more inviting than fresh, cotton bed linen. Embroidered and hand-decorated linens can be expensive, so cheat by sewing pretty ribbons along the top edge of a store-bought sheet. Stitch ribbons onto pillow slips to complete the look, using colors that coordinate with the décor of the room.

Skills needed:
- **Measuring**
- **Machine sewing**

MATERIALS

White sheet

3 coordinating lengths of ribbon ⅜in. (1cm), ⅝in. (1.5cm), and 1¼in. (3cm) in width

Sewing thread to match ribbons

EQUIPMENT

Tape measure

Fabric scissors

Pins

Sewing machine

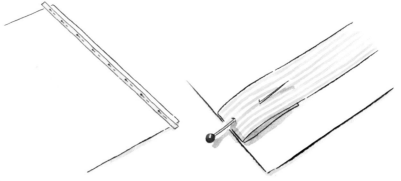

1 Measure the sheet and cut a length of ⅝-in. (1.5-cm) ribbon about 2in. (5cm) longer than the width of the sheet. Pin the ribbon along the top of the sheet ⅝in. (1.5cm) from the edge, folding under 1in. (2.5cm) at each end. Measure from the edge of the sheet to the ribbon as you work to ensure that it's straight. Machine stitch in place.

2 Following Step 1, cut a length of the 1¼in. (3cm) ribbon, pin it across the sheet ¼in. (5mm) below the first, and machine stitch in place.

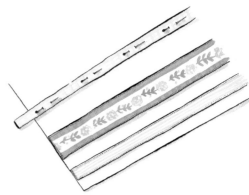

3 Pin the narrowest ribbon across the sheet, ⅝in. (1.5cm) below the second ribbon, and machine stitch as before.

CHAPTER 4

Work AND Play

Drawstring toy bags

You can never have enough storage space for toys and these drawstring bags are both functional and pretty. Made from oddments of fabric sewn together and decorated with a cute fabric flower, you can simply throw toys in them at the end of the day and hang them on a peg rail. They would work equally well for storing gym kit or ballet shoes.

Skills needed:

- **Machine sewing seams**
- **Trimming corners**
- **Using a template**
- **Sewing on buttons**

MATERIALS
10in. (25cm) of 3 coordinating fabrics
Sewing thread to match fabrics
20in. (50cm) of backing fabric
18in. (45cm) of 3 coordinating ribbons
50in. (125cm) of cord
Scraps of fabric
Button 1¼in. (3cm) in diameter

EQUIPMENT
Tape measure
Fabric scissors
Pins
Sewing machine
Sewing needle
Iron

SEAMS
Take ⅝-in. (1.5-cm) seam allowances throughout unless otherwise stated.

1 Cut a 17½ x 7-in. (45 x 17.5-cm) piece of each of the three coordinating fabrics. With right sides together, pin and machine stitch them together along their long edges. Press the seams open. Machine stitch one ribbon over each seam on the right side. Press.

2 Cut a 20 x 17½-in. (50 x 45-cm) piece of fabric for the back of the bag. With right sides together, pin and machine stitch the front and back together, leaving 2¾in. (7cm) unstitched at the top of one side. Turn back the unstitched part of the side edges, so that it's level with the stitching, and press. Trim the corners at the base of the bag to reduce bulk. Fold the top of the bag over by ⅜in. (1cm) and again by 1¼in. (3cm). Machine stitch close to the folded edge to create a channel, then turn the bag right side out.

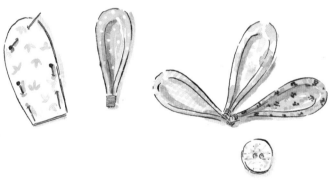

3 Cut two 8-in. (20-cm) lengths of ribbon and machine stitch together to create a double thickness. Stitch onto the middle of the back of the bag, just below the channel, folding the ends under by ⅜in. (1cm). Thread the cord through the channel. Cut two 2¾ x 3-in. (7 x 8-cm) rectangles of fabric. With wrong sides together, fold each piece in half widthwise and machine stitch along both sides. Turn right side out and turn under the top edge by ⅜in. (1cm). Push the ends of the cord into this pocket, and machine stitch along the top.

4 Using the template on page 93, cut two petal shapes from each of five different fabrics. Pin each pair together and machine stitch around the edge, leaving a small gap for turning. Turn right side out and make a few small stitches to gather at the end. Stitch the five petals together to form a flower, and hand stitch to the bag, with a button in the center. Attach the tip of each petal to the bag by making a few small stitches at the back.

Fabric-covered storage box

This is a great storage solution for a home office. Make a whole range in different sizes to keep stationery or correspondence close at hand.

Skills needed:

- **Machine sewing seams**
- **Box stitching**
- **Trimming corners**
- **Slipstitching**

MATERIALS
2 coordinating fabrics

Sewing thread to match fabrics

EQUIPMENT
Tape measure

Fabric scissors

Pins

Sewing machine

Iron

Thick cardboard

Craft knife, steel rule, and cutting mat

Sewing needle

FABRIC QUANTITIES AND CUTTING
Decide how tall and wide you want the box to be. Add the lengths of all four sides together, and then add 1¼in. (3cm). Next, add 1¼in. (3cm) to the height of the sides. Cut a strip of the outer fabric to these dimensions. Take the measurement for the box base and add 1¼in. (3cm) to both the width and the length, then cut another piece of the outer fabric to this size for the base.

SEAMS
Take ⅝-in. (1.5-cm) seam allowances throughout unless otherwise stated.

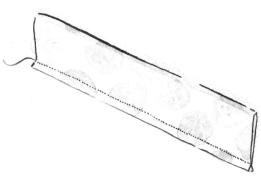

1 To make the handle, cut a 6 x 3-in. (15 x 7.5-cm) rectangle of the outer fabric. Fold it in half lengthwise, pin, and machine stitch along the long raw edge. Turn right side out and press. Fold the ends under by ⅝in. (1.5cm) and press.

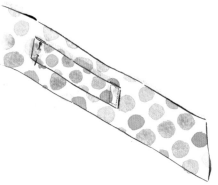

2 Measure ⅝in. (1.5cm) from one end of the strip of fabric you have cut for the sides of the box, and mark with a pin. Measure the width of one end of the box from this mark. Pin on the handle evenly spaced between these two points and machine stitch a square at each end.

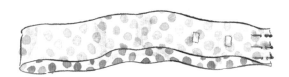

3 With right sides together, pin and machine stitch the short ends of the strip together. Press the seam open.

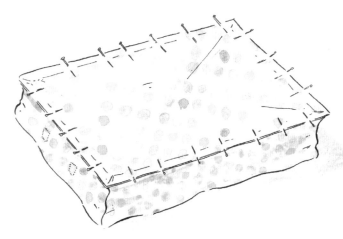

4 With right sides together, pin and machine stitch the side piece to the base piece, making sure that the handle is positioned centrally along one short side.

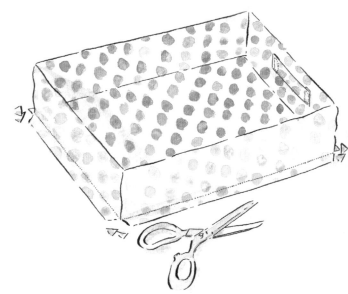

5 Snip the corners to reduce bulk and press all the seams open.

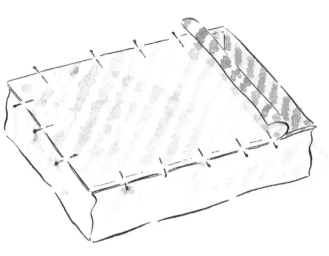

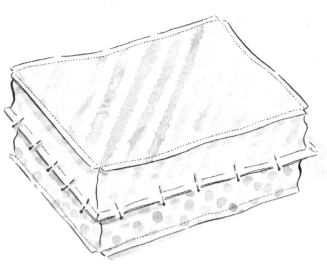

6 Cut out the lining for the sides and base of the box from your coordinating fabric, using the same measurements as before (see box on page 78). With right sides together, pin and machine stitch the short ends of the strip together, and press the seam open. With right sides together, pin and machine stitch the side strip to the base, leaving one short side open. Snip the corners and press the seams open.

7 With right sides together, pin and machine stitch the two fabric box shapes together, leaving one short end open. Press the seam open and turn right side out. Form a box shape with the lining on the inside.

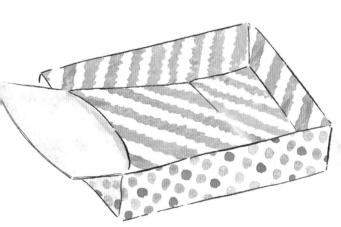

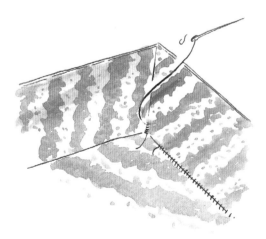

8 Cut out a rectangle of cardboard to fit the base of the box. Insert it into the base of the box through the unstitched opening. Measure and cut two pieces of cardboard for the long sides and two for the short sides. Slot the longer pieces into the sides of the fabric box and the shorter lengths into the ends.

9 Slipstitch the open end closed. Make a few small stitches at each corner through all the layers to hold the lining in place.

Floor pillow

Make a pile of these comfy floor pillows to sink into with a good book or to provide extra seating when guests come to visit. Use two different fabrics for each pillow and cover the button at the center of each pillow with a coordinating fabric for extra interest. The covers cannot be taken off without removing the buttons, so make sure you use pillow forms that are machine washable so that you can throw the whole thing into the machine for easy cleaning.

Skills needed:

● **Machine sewing seams** ● **Trimming seams** ● **Slipstitching** ● **Sewing on buttons**

MATERIALS
30in. (75cm) each of 2 coordinating fabrics

Sewing thread to match fabrics

25½-in. (65-cm) square pillow form

2 self-cover buttons 1¼in. (3cm) in diameter

EQUIPMENT
Tape measure

Fabric scissors

Pins

Sewing machine

Iron

Sewing needle

Upholstery thread and needle

MEASUREMENTS
25½ x 25½in. (65 x 65cm)

SEAMS
Take ⅝-in. (1.5-cm) seam allowances throughout unless otherwise stated.

1 Cut a 26¾-in. (68-cm) square of each fabric. Lay one square right side up on your work surface and place the second one right side down on top of it, aligning all edges. Pin and machine stitch all around, leaving a gap of about 12in. (30cm) in one side. Trim the corners close to the stitching to reduce the bulk.

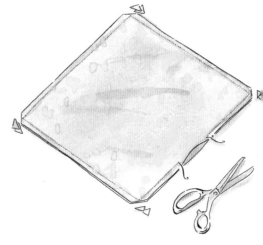

2 Turn the cover right side out and press. Insert the pillow form and slipstitch the opening closed, using small stitches. Find the center point of the pillow cover on both sides and mark with a pin.

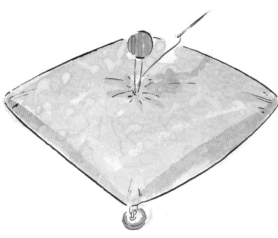

3 Following the manufacturer's instructions, cover the buttons with fabric. Thread an upholstery needle and knot the thread. Stitch through the pillow at the central pin and thread on a button. Take the needle back though the pillow and thread a button onto the other side. Pull the thread firmly to pull the buttons into the pillow. Stitch back through the buttons a couple of times and secure with a few stitches.

Knitting bag

Every crafter needs a knitting bag to hold balls of yarn and knitting needles, but many commercially available versions are more practical than decorative. This stylish bag is roomy enough to hold plenty of yarn and looks good as well. Interfacing has been used to make the fabric as stiff as possible so that it holds its shape, and all the layers are quilted to create a sturdy bag.

Skills needed:

- **Machine sewing seams**
- **Topstitching**
- **Notching or clipping circular seams**
- **Slipstitching**
- **Sewing on buttons**

MATERIALS

40 x 12in. (100 x 30cm) of plain white cotton fabric

40 x 12in. (100 x 30cm) of batting (wadding)

30 x 15in. (75 x 38cm) of patterned fabric

Sewing thread to match fabrics

40 x 14in. (100 x 35cm) of solid-colored fabric

Fusible interfacing

2 buttons

EQUIPMENT

Tape measure

Fabric scissors

Pins

Masking tape

Sewing machine

Iron

Sewing needle

SEAMS

Take ⅝-in. (1.5-cm) seam allowances throughout unless otherwise stated.

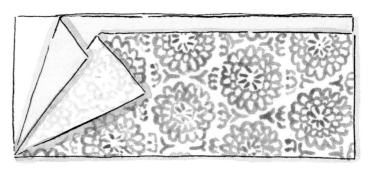

1 Measure and cut a piece of white cotton fabric and a piece of batting (wadding) 30 x 12in. (75 x 30cm). Measure and cut a rectangle of patterned fabric 30 x 11in. (75 x 28cm). Lay the white cotton on the work surface with the batting (wadding) on top of this. Place the patterned fabric rectangle, right side up, onto this, lining up the bottom edges together. Pin the layers together.

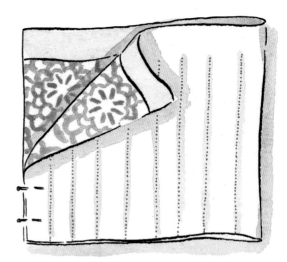

2 Stick a strip of masking tape vertically from the bottom to the top of the fabrics. Measure 1½in. (4cm) from the left-hand side of the tape, sticking another strip of tape parallel to the first. Continue at 1½-in. (4-cm) increments, measuring from the left-hand side of the tape, all the way along the fabric. Machine stitch along the left-hand side of each length of tape to quilt the fabric.

3 With patterned fabric right sides together fold the panel over, lining up along both short sides. Pin and stitch along the edge, and press the seam open.

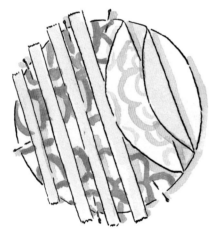

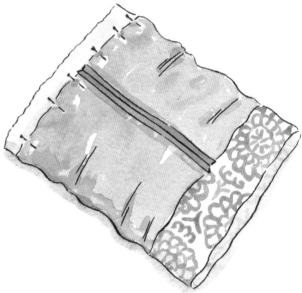

4 Cut circles of white cotton, batting (wadding), and patterned fabric, all with a diameter of 9½in. (24cm). Lay the white cotton onto the work surface with the batting on top of this. Place the patterned fabric circle on the top, right side up. Pin the layers together. Stick a length of tape across the circle and measure and stick parallel strips on either side of the first at 1½-in. (4-cm) increments as before, across the width of the circle. Machine stitch along one side of each length of tape.

5 Measure and cut a piece of the solid-colored fabric 30 x 13½in. (75 x 34cm). With right sides together (if there is a right and wrong side), pin and stitch both short sides together. Place this over the quilted tube, right side out, with the top raw edge lining up with the raw edge of the patterned fabric. Pin and stitch the plain fabric onto the quilted tube.

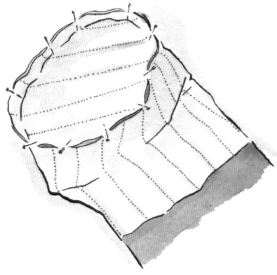

6 With right sides together, pin and stitch the circular base to the main part of the bag. Turn the bag the right way out and push the lining inside. Press the top edge of the lining to form a neat edge. Topstitch around the top and bottom of the cuff.

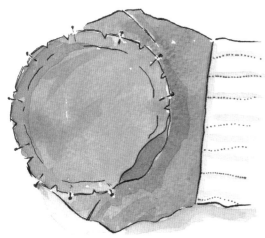

7 Cut a circle of solid-colored fabric for the base of the lining the same size as before. Turn the bag wrong side out again. With right sides together, if applicable, pin and stitch the base to the main lining piece, leaving an opening of about 4in. (10cm). Make small snips around the seam allowance and turn the bag the right way out through the gap in the lining. Slipstitch the opening in the lining closed, and push the lining into the bag.

8 Cut a strip of patterned fabric 23 x 4in. (58 x 10cm). Cut a piece of interfacing to the same size and, following the manufacturer's instructions, press with the iron to attach it to the wrong side of the fabric strip. Fold the strip in half along its length and stitch along one short end and along the length, using a seam allowance of ½in. (1cm). Snip the corners. Turn the tube the right way out and press. Turn the raw end in and topstitch all the way round the handle. Sew the handle onto the bag, finishing with a button at each end of it.

Lined storage basket

This fabric lining is practical as well as pretty, because it prevents delicate items from snagging on the wicker basket. The idea could also be used to line storage baskets for linens, clothing, and even toys.

Skills needed:

- **Calculating measurements**
- **Machine sewing seams**
- **Snipping across corners**

MATERIALS
Basket
Patterned fabric
Sewing thread to match fabric
Ribbon ½in. (15mm) wide

EQUIPMENT
Tape measure
Fabric scissors
Pins
Sewing machine
Iron

SEAMS
Take ⅝-in. (1.5-cm) seam allowances throughout unless otherwise stated.

WORKING OUT FABRIC QUANTITIES
To work out how much fabric you need for the sides of the basket, measure around the top of the outside and add 1¼in. (3cm). Then measure the height and add the amount that you want to fold over to the outside of the basket, plus ⅝in. (1.5cm).

To work out how much fabric you need for the base of the basket, measure along one long edge and add 1¼in. (3cm). Then measure along one short side and add 1¼in. (3cm) to this measurement, too.

You will also need enough ribbon to go all around the top of the basket and the handles, plus 48in. (120cm).

1 Cut a strip of patterned fabric for the sides of the basket (see box, above right). With right sides together, pin the ends together. Place the fabric inside the basket, wrong side out. Check that it fits snugly around the top of the basket, and fold it over to make sure that the lining will not be too tight. Machine stitch the ends together, and press the seam open.

2 Put the lining back into the basket, wrong side out, and press it into the corners with your fingers so that it fits snugly all around. Pin and baste any excess fabric at the corners to form a neat dart. Take the lining out of the basket and machine stitch the corners. (If the sides of your basket are straight, you can omit this step.)

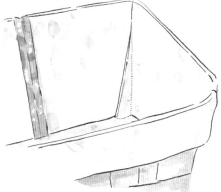

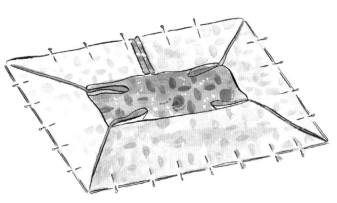

3 Cut a rectangle of fabric for the base of the basket (see Working out fabric quantities, page 88). With right sides together, machine stitch the sides of the lining to the base. Trim across the corners and press.

4 Place the lining inside the basket and mark where the handles are. Cut out a rectangle at each end that is exactly the same size as the handles. Take the lining out of the basket.

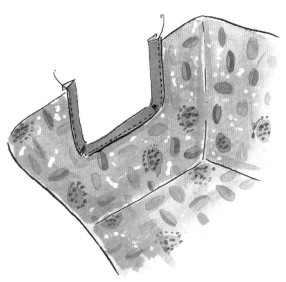

5 For each handle, cut a length of ribbon slightly longer than the sides and base of the handle rectangle and press it in half widthwise. Pin, baste, and machine stitch the ribbon around the handle of the lining, folding the ribbon neatly at the corners.

6 Cut a length of ribbon to fit around one side of the lining plus 24in. (60cm). Press in half widthwise, and pin, baste, and machine stitch it along one side of the lining leaving 12in. (30cm) of ribbon free at each end. Repeat along the other side of the lining. Press and place the lining inside the basket, tying the ribbons with a neat bow at either end.

Templates

Note: some of the templates shown are smaller than actual size and will need enlarging on a photocopier. Where this occurs, the required percentage enlargement is given.

Tea cozy

page 26

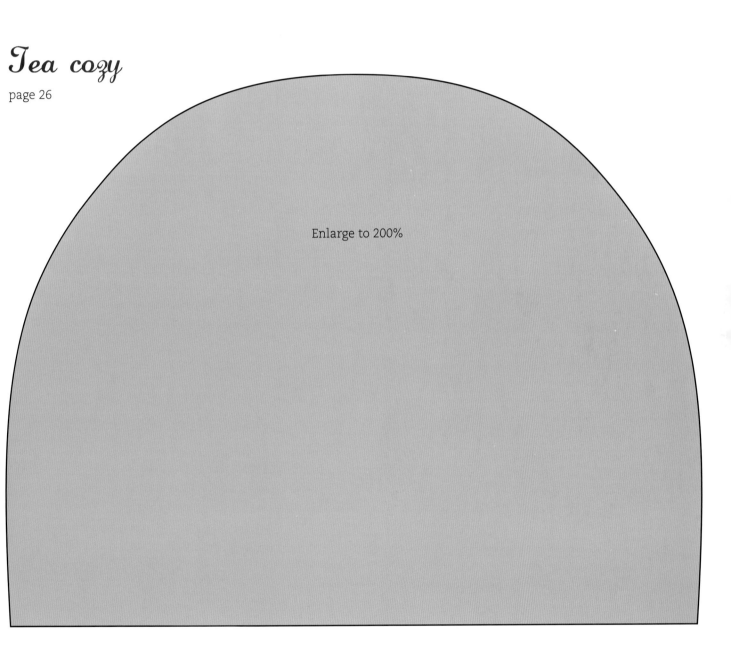

Enlarge to 200%

Peg bag

page 30

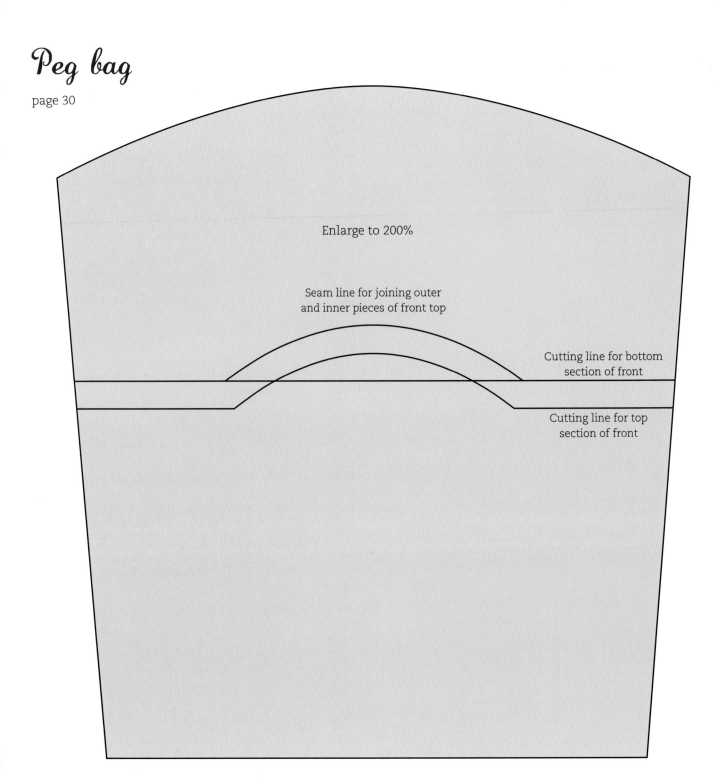

Enlarge to 200%

Seam line for joining outer
and inner pieces of front top

Cutting line for bottom
section of front

Cutting line for top
section of front

Pretty bunting
page 52

Actual size

Actual size

Enlarge to 200%

Actual size

Drawstring toy bags
page 76

Suppliers

UK suppliers

THE BUTTON QUEEN
76 Marylebone Lane
London W1U 2PR
020 7935 1505
www.thebuttonqueen.co.uk

CATH KIDSTON
08450 262 440
www.cathkidston.com

CLOTH HOUSE
47 Berwick Street
London W1F 8SJ
020 7437 5155
www.clothhouse.com

FABRICS GALORE
52–54 Lavender Hill
London SW11 5RH
020 7738 9589
www.fabricsgalore.co.uk

HOBBYCRAFT
0330 026 1400
www.hobbycraft.co.uk

IAN MANKIN
269/273 Wandsworth Bridge Road
London SW6 2TX
020 7722 0997
www.ianmankin.co.uk

JOHN LEWIS
03456 049049
www.johnlewis.com

LAURA ASHLEY
03332 008009
www.lauraashley.com

LIBERTY
Regent Street
London W1B 5AH
020 7734 1234
www.liberty.co.uk

THE LITTLE FABRIC SHOP
14 Beach Station Road
Felixstowe
Suffolk IP11 2DR
01394 273854
www.thelittlefabricshop.co.uk

THE QUILT ROOM
37–39 High Street
Dorking
Surrey RH4 1AR
01306 877307
www.quiltroom.co.uk

TIKKI PATCHWORK
293 Sandycombe Road
Kew
Surrey TW9 3LU
020 8948 8462
www.tikkilondon.com

VV ROULEAUX
102 Marylebone Lane
London W1U 2QD
020 7224 5179
www.vvrouleaux.com

US suppliers

AMY BUTLER
740 587 2841
www.amybutlerdesign.com

BRITEX FABRICS
146 Geary Street
San Francisco
CA 94108
415 392 2910
www.britexfabrics.com

CIA'S PALETTE
4155 Grand Ave S.
Minneapolis
MN 55409
612 823 5558
www.ciaspalette.com

JOANN FABRIC AND CRAFT STORES
www.joann.com

MICHAELS
www.michaels.com

PURL SOHO
459 Broome Street
New York
NY 10013
212 420 8796
www.purlsoho.com

TINSEL TRADING COMPANY
828 Lexington Avenue
New York
NY 10065
212 730 1030
www.tinseltrading.com

Index

Acknowledgments

I would like to thank everyone who worked on this book, especially Debbie Patterson for the beautiful photography and for making the shoots a lot of fun, Marie Clayton for editing the book with such calm and patience, Michael Hill for the lovely illustrations, and Alison Fenton for the great design. At CICO, I would like to thank Sally Powell for all her assistance and support, and Cindy Richards for giving me the opportunity to do the book. You have all helped to make it a really enjoyable project.

Thank you to Maria Dahl for the loan of some lovely props. And thank you, thank you, thank you to Laurie for sharing our home with piles and piles of fabric, ribbons, and buttons and still being enthusiastic about the whole project. A huge thank you to Gracie and Betty, my gorgeous girls, for giving me so many great ideas and lots of inspiration and for getting as excited about fabrics, haberdashery, and making things as I do. You are stars!